SCHIZOPHRENIA

SCHIZOPHRENIA

ONE MAN'S STRUGGLE

RAYMOND EDGELL

authorHOUSE®

AuthorHouse™
1663 Liberty Drive
Bloomington, IN 47403
www.authorhouse.com
Phone: 1-800-839-8640

Published by AuthorHouse   07/27/2012

ISBN: 978-1-4772-5427-1 (sc)
ISBN: 978-1-4772-5426-4 (e)

Library of Congress Control Number: 2012913731

This book is dedicated to the memory of Bruce "Rusty" and Lisa Rutherford.

CONTENTS

INTRODUCTION

I find writing factual details of my life somewhat difficult to do. I've never been the type of person to be embarrassed from my actions, but I did notice while proofreading this book that it is disturbing. I guarantee you all these events actually took place. They were not wild, imaginary mental problems or drug-induced visions.

I am not afraid of the reactions people may have or the way they will look at me in the future. I admit I have done terrible things but feel I need to bring them out to determine the root cause of my schizophrenia. I have always had the love of God, which surpasses all things, and he will lead, guide, and direct me in the coming years. My past is behind me, and I look forward to overcoming this disease. I welcome comments on this book. You will find my e-mail address to be rredgell@ yahoo.com. Hopefully this book can help some people avoid this disease by examining my life and avoiding the same mistakes. Those currently suffering from schizophrenia may find some answers to their own situations. I believe God, through faith in Christ Jesus, is the only cure.

I was watching an episode of *In Touch with Dr. Charles Stanley* one Sunday morning at ten o'clock. I was debating whether to get up and shave to attend church at 10:45. I was very interested in the show and didn't want to miss it by shaving. So I put on a pot of coffee, lit up a smoke, and started typing this book while listening to Dr. Stanley in the background.

His session was about trials in a person's life and what they mean. I have to tell you Charles Stanley has great wisdom from God. He speaks so clearly the Word. He explains it in great detail so you can grasp it. I put him right up there with my own Baptist preacher, Jason Duree. Jason also has great wisdom, and his manner of speaking makes me desire to hear the truth of the Word of God every Sunday. Wisdom can be defined as "seeing God's viewpoint on all matters and responding according to Scripture." I always wondered exactly how to define the word *wisdom*. Thanks, Dr. Stanley.

I have read the Bible every day for nearly eight years now. It is part of my daily routine. I start at Genesis and read every word through Revelation, and then I start over. I heard when I was young that there is great wealth that comes from reading the Bible on a daily basis. I now believe it's true. Brother Jason taught his congregation through God's inspiration that you not only have to read God's Word on a daily basis but also must write it in your heart.

I have asked for wisdom from God on many occasions and feel that he has blessed me with it. I'm writing this book to explain a terrible trial in my life that I count as all joy, which is suffering from schizophrenia. Oh, I still have it. I deal with it 24/7. As a matter of fact, the voices that seem to lie so much promised they would help me write this book. They may be lying, but I believe they or the Holy Spirit will assist me. This will be a factual story of my life before and after the onset of schizophrenia. It will be an attempt to help those suffering with it and possibly doctors who treat it. I hope this also shows the world the power of God, Jesus, and the Holy Spirit in one sinner's life.

Although I'm not 100 percent cured from this disease, I feel it will happen. If not, I count it as joy to suffer through it under God's care and a little medication. I take GEODON. It might not cure my disease, but I can't sleep without it. It may have something to do with the voices being less intense. Maybe not.

My mind is not my own. I feel no one's is really. It is very possible, and most likely, that thoughts are being placed in there by the spirit world. I believe this happens to all people on earth; they just don't sense it. Look at how far computers have advanced in the last ten years, and consider where they will be in another ten years. I believe God is at the keyboard of the most powerful computer. A person's brain is like a super computer. It may be possible that spirits interface with our brains computer. The difference with schizophrenia is that we can hear out loud those thoughts at the same time they are placed in the mind by whatever spirit has been appointed to do so. It happens simultaneously, so I can't discern if the thoughts are being generated by my mind or from the voices I hear. They know every thought I have at the exact millisecond I think it. In other words, as I'm thinking it, they are saying it. But they also say things that I'm not thinking, so I know it is not a mental problem. They usually begin by starting a sentence, and my mind completes the sentence with their voices in sync with my thoughts.

The spirits that are in my mind are always tuned in to my thoughts. The slightest thought I have that leads me searching for their voice produces an immediate response. If I divert my thoughts to them from the corners of my mind for a split second, they pick up on that impulse and begin speaking. During periods when their barrage of attacks become too much, I often recite in my mind the phrase "Jesus Jesus precious Jesus". I say this over and over sometimes for what seems like hours. It helps greatly. They never say anything important. They don't tell me to harm anyone either. It seems they just don't want me to do any thinking of my own. Sometimes I ask the spirits if Jesus Christ came in the flesh to determine if the spirits or voices in my head are of the antichrist. 1st John Ch. 4 tells that if the spirits confess not that Jesus came in the flesh then they are of the antichrist. One voice often answers with yes, Jesus came in the flesh. The problem is there are always two voices in my head. One, I feel, is continuously lying and the other telling the truth. I can't tell which is which. I believe they are doing Gods will in tormenting me in this manner.

The Holy Spirit also resides in the heart of all God's children. In the book of Luke, chapter 1, Zacharias tells that his son John shall be a prophet and prepare the way for the Lord. Zacharias said this at the time of John's circumcision when he was eight days old. How did Zacharias know the future? God controls time, and most thoughts must be placed in the mind by spirits. For some reason that I don't understand, there are both good and bad thoughts. We must determine the right course of action based on the Holy Spirit residing in us. Our minds have thousands of inputs daily. We have to react to each one of them. The Holy Spirit helps me sort out the lies and truths told to me in my thought process, and I react. I'll try to make sense of this by an examination of my life. You will see from my career path that I am a logical-thinking person. My experience was an awful and powerful one that was imputed toward me in a disturbing manner. It ultimately drove this sane, forty-year-old man who never had had thoughts of suicide to attempt it.

CHAPTER 1

MY ADDICTION BEGINS

I was born and currently reside in a small town in southwest Oklahoma. I spent many years away from my hometown but was drawn back by recent events. My dad was in the air force, and we have a base here. My mom was a local girl. She was thirteen when she got pregnant with me, and my dad was seventeen. Kind of young but they were in love. I now visit my mom every morning to dispense her medication and have coffee. We listen to a local radio show called "Swap Shop" every morning, which presents garage sales and other buy-and-sell opportunities. I stay with her for between a half-hour to an hour every day. We enjoy eating a light breakfast together and drinking exotic coffees while chatting and making plans for the coming day.

My mom has a little problem of speaking whatever is on her mind. She can't help it. Whatever she is thinking, she talks. It drives me crazy because I, of course, have schizophrenia. I keep telling her to stop because I can't take any more inputs to my brain. She does her best but still bombards me with her tales. She talks about when I was a baby. There was nothing out of the ordinary; I was a normal child. My dad married her, and I had three younger sisters. We were poor, but my dad always found a way to provide. I had a wonderful childhood with lots of trips to theme parks, Easter egg hunts, and great Christmases. There were periods of the family as a whole going to church.

I never knew we were poor. We had lots of love in the home, and visiting the grandparents was a weekly thing. My dad somehow rented a log cabin at the lake when I was about twelve and a half or thirteen. We camped there for two weeks. We enjoyed shimmy-board riding and the whole scene. Then when we were leaving, I was the last to step off the beach. I spied this girl with humongous knockers for a twelve- or thirteen-year-old. I later dated her when I was a senior and she had graduated the year before. I got the biggest hard-on I could imagine.

That is where the trouble started. Sex would consume most of my thoughts for the next twenty-seven years. I know now that I have what is clinically called acute addiction disorder. The beach incident was in the early '70s. Who knew?

I spent the next twenty-seven years with a sex problem. I had many women during my life—more than is normal, I would guess—but masturbation was always my mainstay. I preferred it over women. There was something about that release so that I just wanted to do it again and again.

I consider myself having a highly addictive personality in many areas. I find myself wondering how Jesus dealt with his sexual urges. He was a man, after all. I know he led a sinless life so he didn't lust after women, because it says in Matthew 5:28, "But I say unto you, that whosoever looketh on a woman to lust after her hath committed adultery with her already in his heart."

Adultery is definitely a sin, so how did he deal with his sexual urges? Did he masturbate? I guess it is something we each have to deal with on a personal level. I'm under the belief that everyone does it. It seemed normal for me to do it. I do feel I was excessive though. I have learned to put away my lustful desires. I have not been with a woman in over eight years. I went about a year without masturbating and now only do it once every three or four months. I still feel guilty about doing it but tell myself that I'm not sure it is a sin. I mean, is the naked woman I'm masturbating to even married?

What does Jesus do? My faith tells me he is alive today in the form of a man. Since he is a man, it seems like he would have to go to the restroom daily and have a sexual release now and then. No one on earth has the answer to this profound question, and the voices I hear aren't talking. I can't believe what the voices say anyway. I've caught them in numerous lies. And just as in the story of the boy who cried wolf, I can't believe anything they say now.

As you read later in this book, you will understand the steps I've taken to get where I am dealing with the schizophrenia in my life. I just wanted you to know that these steps are key to living with it, and I'm under the impression it will end altogether after this book is published. I believe in many profound statements by man and every word in the Bible. All things work for the greater good of God. Schizophrenia, while devastating, is for the greater good of God. It is one of his ways of correcting his children.

CHAPTER 2

TIME DEFINED

My parents divorced when I was fourteen. My mom was young and wanted to be free, and my dad had a childhood sweetheart in Houston. He left and my mom tried to keep us kids together, but we got dispersed. I stayed with my alcoholic grandpa and saintly grandmother until I graduated from high school.

During my eleventh-grade psychology class, I distinctly recall two things. The first was my teacher saying, "Look around; 10 percent of this class will be institutionalized for a mental problem." I was so smart. I said, "It definitely ain't me."

And the second thing I recall is the teacher posing a question. He wanted everyone to get out a sheet of paper and write down the definition of time. Somehow I came up with the right answer he was looking for. I answered, "Is." I was the only one who ever got it right in his class. It took me about five to seven years—I don't recall exactly—until I reexamined the question and came up with the real answer that is longer than one word.

When I was twenty-one, I entered the National Guard. My position or job classification was "computer," which was officially 13E. This was the early '80s before *real* computers. My job was to calculate firing data coordinates for the howitzers by using charts and darts. Later I worked with FADAC ("Freddie"), a large mainframe computer. In calculating data, a circle represents 360 degrees. But the military classifies degrees as mills, and they range from 0-6,400. My church experiences as a youth taught me Alpha and Omega, the beginning and the end, so I used those for the 0-6,400 respectfully. There is an end and a beginning to everything except God. He is infinite and so are his children who find Jesus as their Lord and Savior. Time *is* being interpreted as a fractal part of a space between two mills in the circle of life from this exact moment and since time began.

Time is God pointing to a split second between two mills. Then he will freeze that time and examine the goings-on of everyone in that moment. It is easy to see if you draw it out on a sheet of paper in the form of a chart. This seems likely how God will judge the world, because he is the only power that determines time. How could he judge everyone's actions to the split second if he didn't know what time it was? You might be surprised at how many of my classmates wrote down the time of 2:27.

A schizophrenic's perception of time may be part of his illness. Take for instance, a senseless act done by the person with the disease. He may not be able to tell you when he did it. He may even deny that it ever happened. To him, the act was lost in time. He might claim that someone else must have done the act. As time goes by entropy or chaos increases in the schizophrenics mind. His perception of events decreases. Since no time occurred for this event to happen in his mind, will God judge him for those acts? This type of schizophrenic is the most dangerous.

I had done some drugs while staying with my grandparents and acquired a taste for alcohol. It was nothing serious, but when I was a senior at age sixteen I had a beard and the drinking age was eighteen in Oklahoma. I didn't have a first-hour class so every school day I would wait for 8:10 to come around and then get me a quart of beer at the local 7-Eleven. There were no school officials in parking lots in those days, and I would drink my quart while popping one of my grandma's Darvon's and listening to Aerosmith eight-tracks. I would then go into class and make straight A's.

Life didn't seem fair to me, and I dreamed of the future like any kid. But soon I realized I had no financial means to go to college even with straight A's. That's when my uncle offered me a place in OKC to start my life. My dad gave me my first car when I was sixteen, and I graduated early at seventeen. He made a twelve-hour trip to deliver the car. I was both grateful and amazed.

I moved to Oklahoma City the day after graduation. I stayed with my uncle for a few months. I got a good job then got an apartment with a coworker. I worked in an office-furniture warehouse in downtown OKC. In a few months I was made manager. A friend wrecked the car my dad had given me, so I got a 1970 Camaro Rally Sport and went on a tear!

CHAPTER 3

OKLAHOMA CITY

One rainy night, I was driving down a major road in south OKC and was right next to Mathis Brothers Furniture. I lived about a half mile down Walker Street in some roach-infested apartment complex. It had just started to rain, and I punched the gas just before getting to the intersection. The light was red, and I did a 360 in the street. I ended up perfectly parked in the turning lane where I should be to make the turn. I waited for the light to turn green and headed toward the apartment. My friend and I decided to hit another bar farther down the road and back to the west. We drank a few more pitchers of beer and headed home again through the same intersection. I did the same thing as before and made a perfect stop, coming out of the 360. Then I headed home.

I looked back and police lights were in my rearview window. I drove the extra block and parked in our lot at the apartments, and then the cops got out and came up to me. They harassed me a little about not stopping when they hit the lights, but they were so amazed at the two perfect 360s that they said they had never seen anything like it and just wanted to talk to me. They were parked in the Mathis Brothers lot for quite a while and saw both of them. I thought I was getting a DUI, but they just laughed and left.

I added this to the story to let you examine for yourself if drugs or alcohol had any part in me developing schizophrenia. I've had seven DUIs, but never once was I out of control. In my youth, I just liked to go out on the weekends, and that is when the cops are looking for drunk drivers. The police are supposed to be there to protect and to serve. I believe the main reason for police patrolling the streets is for the vast source of revenues a DUI gives the state. I don't condone drinking and driving; it's just that the tests for determining one's level of being able to control a motor vehicle are not individually based, as they should be. We each have different tolerance levels, and mine is very high. I believe I can drive satisfactorily at a blood-alcohol level of 2.0. The law is the law and I paid all my fines, but I never had a wreck.

It's strange right now while writing this, but the voices are quieter than normal. They have been on a low key for a couple of years now, but this is below the normal level of confusion. I think I will continue.

My friend Terry Warden, who I lived with a short while, was a character. He had an ugly '66 Mustang, but it ran like a bat out of hell. I had my '70 Camaro, and we decided to have a contest to see how many different women we could pick up and sleep with in a seven-day period. It was state fair week in Oklahoma and the pickings were ripe.

On day one, we found a couple of women who were traveling through town and had their own hotel room. Those were the first ones. He beat me by a half. I had four and a virgin that I didn't get to complete, so I count it as a half. And he had five. Oh, well. He won. He soon got back with his real girlfriend, and I was left alone in the roach-infested, one-bedroom apartment. My cousin, Jerry Don, who had just graduated from high school wanted to move up to OKC, and I took him in.

Those were the days. We both had jobs and plenty of women, beer, and marijuana. This was the early '80s in a big city, and Jerry Don still had that small-town attitude. He observed me taking a hit while parked in traffic and went hysterical while saying, "Put it down. Do you want to get caught?" I explained we'd never see those other drivers and passengers again, and in a few seconds he got it! This was long before cell phones and computers.

I remember going over to a friend of my girlfriend's. She had her own Harley and was a beautiful blonde like my girlfriend. She started getting real horny and made an obscene phone call to a radio DJ. She was dancing and grinding when she got the song played, and I said, "Why don't you make a call to my cousin and see how he reacts to your suggestions?" She did, and he knew something was up and didn't masturbate with her.

I sure would have. I had this addictive personality and had been making a few obscene calls of my own. No caller ID in those days. She asked my girlfriend if she could have me, and my girlfriend agreed, to my delight. We had a wild time. An annotation in my Bible says, "There is pleasure in sin for a while, but the end result is death."

It wasn't long before Jerry Don and I moved into a trailer park in Midwest City, Oklahoma. My uncle bought this old trailer and charged us rent. I liked it at first. We met all kinds of people and got a beautiful dog that was a cross of a Lab and a golden retriever. We called her Haze. We got the name from a Neil Young song whose lyrics include "In the yellow haze of the sun."

That was around the time I got my first of seven DUIs. I also got three assault and batteries in a four-week period. They each happened on Fridays, and I had to spend the weekends in jail. I felt I was the victim in the case each time. I'm sure the people who lived in the trailer park were so jealous of me. I had gotten a new 750 Gs Suzuki motorcycle and had my Camaro restored black on the inside and outside. The people who had me arrested were a close-knit bunch of about twenty-five residents of the trailer park. One time a guy almost strangled me to death, but the next-door neighbor kid who was a friend of mine cracked him over the head with a board. Needless to say, with all the jail time, I soon lost my job.

About that same time, my cousin moved to Colorado and left me there. He had this girlfriend who later became his wife. One time before he moved out, he was gone and she came over and wanted to stay in his room for a night. I said that was fine. It was cold in the trailer, and I didn't have the heat on because I was broke. I had this exquisite California king water bed that was heated. She ended up crawling into bed with me to get warm, and a few things led to her touching me. I was leaking a lot of pre-seminal fluid and she was amazed at how much; she knew I was turned on, so we had a onetime thing. A few years later, when they were married, I was staying a night with them and he ran down the street to the store. As soon as he left, she came in and kissed me. I didn't know what to think. He would only be gone a few minutes, and we didn't do anything else. He ended up separating from her a few years later and then getting back with her. He knew she was sleeping around. I narrowly escaped the sin of adultery. I have done my best to avoid adultery in my life. I'm pretty sure I've done it a few times without realizing, but I feel righteous for the many times I said no to it.

CHAPTER 4

NATIONAL GUARD DAYS

Without a job, I decided to move back to my hometown. I toiled for a while doing very little and stayed with my mom in a trailer, and then I stayed with her in a motel/apartment complex. I also stayed with my grandparents often. I had a few meaningless jobs and just did normal things. I was staying the night at my best friend's dad's apartment. He was a base fireman and stayed at the air base most of the time.

My best friend and I had a little powwow about our future. We thought of joining the coast guard, and we almost did. At the last moment, we decided to join the National Guard and get college tuition. Sounded like a good idea, so we went and inquired. I was twenty-one and soon headed off to basic training.

The National Guard split us up because of our military occupational specialties, as determined by our aptitude tests. He became an 82C surveyor and I was a 13E computer. We did go to the same base at the same time but were in different areas. I think I saw him once the entire four months of basic.

The base was only sixty miles away from my hometown, and I had gotten into a little trouble with the law right before I was to leave for training. The army was made aware of it, and I was allowed to leave for one night to attend trial. I had five charges stemming from an incident at a convenience store and a slight fender bender in a separate parking lot. I told my bunk buddy—his last name was the same as mine except I had two ll's at the end so we were buddies—that I was going and we came up with a plan to smuggle some marijuana. We planned it all out. I took out a two-inch area of the seams of my cap and placed about a quarter-ounce bag of marijuana in there. We had running privileges around the complex with no drill sergeant, and there was a secluded spot with a grove of trees. We would drop out of the run and hit the woods, smoke a little, and take another lap. Good times.

At this time I didn't smoke cigarettes—just a lot of pot. A few years later, the price of pot shot up and I decided to quit. I have probably smoked three puffs over the last twenty-five years. The one thing I regret that I got from my basic training was the cigarette habit. We were standing at rest at the pay barn, and the drill instructor said, "Smoke 'em if you got 'em." I remember his exact words. A buddy offered me one, and I was hooked. The calm that came over me was amazing. I mean I was so tired because we ran like three miles every day and did all those push-ups. The cigarette made my day. When we got back to the barracks, the same buddy decided to quit and gave me a couple of cartons.

Anyway back to the court proceedings. The military had rubbed off on me after only a few weeks, and the judge took note of that. I represented myself. Everyone was there: the store clerk, the cops, the old couple whose car I bumped into with my motorcycle, and my mom. I cross-examined the convenience store clerk and said, "Did I pay for everything?"

She said, "Yes." I then examined the people charging me with hit-and-run and said, "Did I not stop and talk with you, and you said there was nothing to worry about?" He agreed. Then it was the cop's turn. I don't recall my exact words, but I was found guilty of one thing: disobeying law enforcement by using foul language. I got off on everything else. Apparently you cannot cuss out a cop in Oklahoma. I paid my fine, put my smuggling cap back on, and headed back.

CHAPTER 5

JERRY DON'S ACID TRIP

I skirted the law often as a young man. Nothing I deemed too serious.

There was this one time that my cousin and I went to a Bob Seager concert. I think the statute of limitations on this crime has run out, so I will tell of it. It was at Myriad Botanical Gardens in downtown OKC. I worked about three blocks away, so I asked my boss if I could have the key to the gate to safely lock up my cousin's car. It was a fifteen-foot high fence with barbed wire at the top. I had never taken acid and neither had my cousin, but that night he did.

We had prime seats. Jerry Don had stayed in line all night to get them. For some reason, right after we sat down, he gave me his ticket and left to the convenience stand. Security wouldn't let him back to the seating area. Someone offered him LSD, and he took way too much. Being his first time, it really got him good. He had the keys to the car and the gate where I worked. I looked for him everywhere at the Myriad then rationalized that he may be at the car.

I got to the gate and yelled for what seemed like forever to see if he was sleeping in the car. I saw his head pop up, but he was out of it. There was a cop car in the outer parking lot and an undercover cop car as well. I checked the doors to see if they were unlocked so I could radio for help. The back door was unlocked, and I spied a toolbox in the back seat. I turned and went back to the fence and decided to try to scale it. I did it.

I went to the car, but he had all the doors locked. It took about ten or fifteen more minutes to get him to unlock the door. I threw gravel up in the air and let it fall on the roof. Then I drove out and locked the gate. He was really out of his mind. I don't know why, but I decided to snag the toolbox from the undercover car. I threw it in the backseat and hauled ass home. I looked at everything that was in it: high-tech gadgets the police used for the sex crimes division.

The next morning, I told Jerry Don we'd better take this out to Lake Stanley Draper and bury it in the woods for a few weeks. When we got back, a neighbor said two men in suits were at our trailer and knocking on the door. I guess they got my fingerprints from the door handle. They never came back, and I kept the gadgets for many years. There was a zoom viewer that gave the distance of an object and other things like a diamond-tipped pen.

That was one crazy time in my life.

CHAPTER 6

THE BRIGHT SUN

After basic training, I went back to my hometown and went to junior college. I worked at a convenience store where my mom was manager. I still had my 750 Suzuki and quite often took trips to the lake. We have a lovely state park just seventeen miles north of Altus. There is a little-known cave up in the hills. Someone showed me where it was, and it was just barely navigable by a small dirt bike. I was as reckless as one could be and managed to make it many times there on my large 750.

One time I had something strange happen just outside the cave. I wasn't suicidal but didn't care too much to exist. Anyway, I took some whiskey and other drugs and took the trip up to the cave. Just outside the cave is a small plateau where I could park the bike. It was March and still cold, but the sun was bigger than I had ever seen it. It felt warm and no wind was blowing. I was alone so I took off all my clothes to get an early tan. I had a portable cassette player and was listening to the band Rush. You know the song "Subdivisions," where it says, "Conform or be cast out." I played that over and over. I have a high tolerance to drugs (and pain for that matter). In my younger days, I could recall exactly what happened, but it is a blur now.

The sun was just above the horizon and about two hours from setting. A strange calm came over me, and I stopped listening to the cassette. I took out the earpieces and just stared at the sun. For some reason, I could look deep into it without burning my eyes for what seemed like a half hour. I recall having thoughts that didn't seem like my own, and they were calming, saying everything was okay.

Anyway, I didn't overdose. I got up, put my clothes on, and went to the north shore beach area and raced up and down the beach on my bike. This ended when my intake manifold of the carburetor got clogged with sand. Luckily a biker couple came by in a truck and took me to their cabin. We played poker all night, and I won about forty-five bucks. The next morning, all my stuff was gone except the bike. I had some really nice Harley saddlebags. I guess they got their forty-five bucks worth from me anyway. I managed to get the bike started and headed home. I went to a diner and ate a burger, one of the best I ever had, and that calming sense came back to me: everything in my life was going to be okay.

CHAPTER 7

SUMMER CAMP

Every year the National Guard holds a two week event called "Summer Camp". It is a time for maneuvers and bonding with fellow soldiers. To me it was a lot of fun and a nice paycheck. I got my first and only sexually transmitted disease while on my first two week camp. Actually it happened just before camp but the symptoms didn't take hold until after a few days of training. They took me to an army doctor who put a swab into my penis to get a culture sample, man did that hurt. It turned out to be the clap or gonorrhea. The night I got it was something else. My buddy Bryon and I had done some work on an old 62 Pontiac Catalina rag top. You know the style, the one that is as big as a boat. It had whale tails and could seat up to ten when the top was down. The owner was so grateful she let us cruise it for the weekend. My fourteen year old cousin got all her friends together and we cruised the night away. I guess I was twenty-two at this time. When it was time to crash we dropped all the girls off and went to Bryon's dads' apartment. Another good friend, Kenton, decided to stay the night with us. They were both pretty tired and went to crash in the bedroom. I stayed in the living room to sleep on the couch. I wasn't tired and was watching television. I heard a knock on the door. It was one of my cousin's girlfriends that we had just dropped off. She had been having a tough time in her life. She had run away from her mom and was living with her boyfriend. I guess they had an argument or something because there she was. She was like a nymph, very petit and slim. I couldn't get enough and we had sex many times that night with my friends fast asleep in the next room. She left before daylight. I told my buddy's and they said no way. I just smiled. I paid dearly for that night during the two weeks of summer camp.

The next year, as my second summer camp was coming to a close, the talk in the barracks was that they were holding interviews for O.C. S., Officer Candidate School. The main reason I went to the interview was to get an extension of two more weeks pay for the summer. I was already scheduled to go to N.C. O. School the following week after camp. I figured this would give me six or seven weeks full time military pay and set my bank account up nicely for the remainder of the summer. I walked in to the interview and went immediately into a parade rest stance looking straight ahead. The colonel said. "I'm going to ask you just one question" He went on to say, answer it without delay. "The quicker you give me the answer the better your answer will look to me". He asked me if I was ready for the question and I said, Sir Yes Sir. He asked me to solve the equation of thirty percent of ninety. I knew it was a math question when I heard thir . . . so I formed the answer the exact millisecond after he said ninety. I responded with twenty-seven the moment he finished the question. He and the three or four officers in the room were very impressed and I was immediately given the candidacy. I completed the two week program but in order to become an officer you had to also attend one weekend a month for almost a year. I was attending and doing well up until the halfway point. The instructors found out, through police records, that I had two D.U.I's. They said I could remain in the course and possibly graduate if I gave a speech in front of the class of candidates explaining the evils and pitfalls of drinking and driving. I knew I couldn't be honest and appease the training officers at the same time so I simply bowed out of the course. Once during that two week training camp we were all in the showers. You had to do everything quickly so a buddy and I were sharing a smoke. This one candidate looked at me and said. "A body like that and you are smoking?" He was a short and slight fellow. I thought he was gay and didn't answer him but I kept his words in my thoughts.

CHAPTER 8

KISSING COUSINS

A few other noteworthy things happened during this period of my life. I was still in junior college and staying with my mom at the apartment complex /motel. Two girls were living in the complex as well. I didn't know it at the time, but they were my third cousins. I dated one and then the other and would visit them often with my other best friend, Arthur. We would on occasion go to his rented house, which was his first place away from his parents. His parents owned a glass business in Altus. We spent many a night in the workplace afterhours, making wooden one-hitters on the wet, belt-driven sander.

Everything changed with our friendship one night. I was looking for him and went to his house on my motorcycle. He wasn't home, but at the same time my cousin, Danny, came by his house and we decided to go to the rundown shack another friend and I had just rented for some strange reason.

I think I might have stayed there a total of two nights in all. While we were out at the place, which was about three miles from town, someone broke into Arthur's house. He had this airplane nose cone that he had made into a coffee table with a hole in the center. It probably contained $ 500 worth of change. I had jumped in the truck with my cousin and left my bike in Arthur's yard.

Upon my return, he told me what had happened, and I think the police were there. He wanted to go to the girls' apartment because he suspected them. I was somewhat naive and said, "No way." He had some black-tar hashish that was stolen too. So he played it cool at the girls for a while, and then we left. That was the end of our friendship. Somehow he determined that they did do it, which I found out later they did, and he said I was an accomplice because I was throwing him off by saying they didn't do it and putting my motorcycle in his front yard. I've only seen him twice in the many years since then. He was my co-best friend, and I lost him. I saw him once at my grandmother's funeral and once at his mom's funeral. I told him both times I had nothing to do with it, and I feel that deep down he blames me still.

One time at the apartment complex, some guys from a roughneck company had a room for a month. One guy was huge and the other guy was slight with many tattoos. Tattoos were illegal in Oklahoma at that time. One night these guys were interested in the two girls I had been seeing. I was leaving the girls' apartment and the guys were coming up drunk. We struck up a conversation, and I could tell the slighter one was upset or jealous of my relationship with the girls.

They invited me to their apartment, and they were both so drunk. The smaller guy got feisty, and I ended up running him through the wall of his room. The big guy backed down and said he was out of it. I left but saw them the next day. The feisty small guy apologized to me, and we struck up a friendship that lasted a couple of weeks until they moved on.

I tell you this because he was a tattoo artist and offered to give me one for free. I hadn't read the Bible at that time and hadn't read the Scripture saying not to tattoo your body. God doesn't like it. I picked out a grim reaper because I decided then and there what it meant to me: fear no one or no thing, not even death. Fear only the Lord, and all will be just fine. I got the tattoo on my back and have taken great pains to keep it covered. I've only talked to one or two people about its meaning. I felt everyone would interpret it wrong if I went shirtless. To me, it is a statement of faith. I just wish I hadn't done it, because of God's commandment not to, so I never show it.

CHAPTER 9

ON MY WAY

I was about twenty-three now and wondering what to do with my life. I moved back to the big city with my uncle and either he said to take a technical college course or I heard it on the radio. I was now on my way to a career. I went to the tech school for nine months. It was the equivalent of two years in college. I didn't learn too much. Like I said earlier, I had an A average in school and it seemed like I could just lay hands on a book and attain the knowledge held within. Even in high school, I never did any homework. I would listen intently to the teacher's instruction and not even bother with the books. I did very well. I graduated in the top of my class, and this particular tech school promised job placement after graduation.

While attending tech school, I was living with a woman who was twice my age and I was working at a store called Payless Cashways as a clerk in the electrical department. We had financial difficulties, and it didn't work out between us. One thing I regret to this day is how it ended. She had given me a bottle of expensive cologne and then took it away. So I was very mad. I moved out, and someone I knew asked if it was okay if he stole her safe she kept in her closet. That man said he would pay my $250-fine to get my license back. I didn't really need it back; I had a legal Oklahoma driver's license in another person's name with my picture on it. But that is another story. I said, "Fine, go ahead." I don't know what was in the safe, but I now had two valid driver's licenses. That theft is one of my biggest regrets in life.

I graduated and took a job in a steel mill as an industrial electrical maintenance technician. I loved it. Great pay for someone who was poor, and in essence it was my job title for my whole adult working life. I was working with hot molten steel running through massive rollers to reduce it down to flat bars. We also made rebar. I was introduced to technology in its' simplest form. We used old school methods of control to drive the processes to produce the steel. I got some valuable training on outdated electronics. My supervisor was a highly intelligent engineer. He told me one day, soon after I was hired on, that all electricians drink beer. He got me started in frequenting bars. We spent many an afternoon in the local pub discussing schematics. We would often design improvements to the mill over the roar of honky-tonk music. Some of our best ideas came from sharing a pitcher of beer.

CHAPTER 10

PASTOR DUREE VISITS

I started the words of this book about nine months ago and was going to forget about it, but the voices and my inner voice, which I believe is the Holy Spirit, said to me, "Finish it." I had determined in my mind not to write it for any other reason except to help those suffering with this disease, and I could not possibly continue without an ending. The voices lead me to believe it will all be over soon after this book is published.

I was busy writing the book today and my pastor and a deacon from my church came over as part of their weekly visitations to the community. He said he decided to visit me tonight because I hadn't been to church in several weeks and that he saw me publicly go to the altar during closing ceremonies at the Church last Sunday.

I decided then, after seven years knowing the pastor, to tell him of my affliction with the disease of schizophrenia. I said when he was about to leave, "I bet you didn't expect to hear that when you came over." He said, "No, I didn't." I knew there would be a prayer after the session, so I told him, "I don't know if I want it to end completely." It almost killed me, but it is so much better. I feel the Lord has turned it into a blessing and wanted him to pray for understanding the meaningless talking the voices do these days.

Honestly, I don't know what to think of this anymore. For so long, I've been going to church most Sundays and helping my family on a daily basis. I feel like it is a blessing. I have a high monthly social security check and checks from my nephew who has lived with me for the last five years. His mother Lisa, my sister, died young, and a year or so later his dad Bruce died. My nephew is autistic, so he gets his dad's social security plus his dad's retirement pay from the air force. Bruce was a twenty-year serviceman. He must have known he was dying but did not elaborate on it when he asked me about six years ago, at age forty-six, to take care of his boys if he died. Alec has a twin brother who is currently in prison. I said, "Sure will," with no hesitation.

At the time, I had just started my social security check coming monthly and knew I could afford to help his boys if it came down to it. I had no idea we would get his dad's social security and retirement. It came as a welcome surprise, a blessing. They each got a hundred-grand death benefit.

I have invested those monies with aid from a financial advisor from my bank that is run by the music director of my church. I bought them a house for rental purposes. It is a multifamily dwelling with three separate living quarters giving them three monthly incomes. For each of my nephews, I put $50,000 into a fund that gives them a monthly dividend of $250 each. I put $20,000 of Andrew's into a savings account so he will have something when he gets out of prison, and I took a strategy of investing about $25,000 of Alec's monies in fine art. The art market is at an all-time low right now. The high-end works are reaching new highs, but lesser works can be bought very inexpensively. I have many fine works of art. The dozen or so that I've sold have made it seem like a nice investment. I have a store on eBay: Ray's Fine Art and More. Search for my store by the username, steadyy. It keeps me busy and gives me something to do in my spare time when I'm not helping out others in my daily routine.

I have three works that I will not sell: a print of Jesus kneeling in the garden of Gethsemane, an Albrecht Durer depiction of Jesus on the cross, and an original Uri Lifschitz lithograph depicting the bust of a man in the throngs of schizophrenia. They all three hang on the wall at the foot of my bed.

Alec's room is adorned with fine works from Looney Tunes and other like art. He is still very young in his mind, even though he is now twenty.

The voices have moved from me to Alec and my mom from time to time. They only attack them one or two days out of a year. Once I find out that the voices are pounding on their minds, I pray to God that the voices leave them alone and double up my suffering in their place. I don't wish for anyone to have this disease; I've learned how to handle it and would rather take the extra intensity.

It starts and ends with God. If you've read the Bible, you may recall a passage where the disciples talk about a demonic spirit they could not expel, and Jesus told them that this kind only comes out by prayer and fasting. I tried prayer and fasting, yet I am powerless over the two spirits that rage in my mind. Jesus commanded the spirit to leave and he is God. In prayer, I often say, "Not my will, Lord, but yours be done." I also give thanks for every meal and morsel of food I am blessed with. Every time I eat without fail!

Another thing I do, because my mom taught me this when I was young, is I hold my breath and say a prayer over every bridge I cross while driving.

Some people say it is a sin to be rich, mainly because Jesus said it is harder for a rich man to enter heaven than a camel to go through the eye of a needle. They definitely have the wrong outlook. It's ok to be rich but you must understand you can't take it with you. The more you give to charity the more blessings the Lord will heap upon you now and in Heaven. God wants us all to be content with food and clothing. The more you have, the more you should give. What more do you really need? He says the birds don't worry about their next meal. God provides. We came into this world with nothing, and we will certainly leave with nothing. How rich is anyone? Happiness in life is doing God's will, and if he blesses you with monies then it is best to give it to those who need it.

I have to say this. In another job I had in the '90s, right when programmable logic controllers (PLCs) were coming out and I was in on the cutting edge of new technology in my career, I was at work one night. I was in a certain room and placed my hand into a railing and pulled out a small Bible. I still hadn't read the Bible at that time and decided to open it to any random page and read one passage. The verse was Ephesians 4:28: "Let he that stole steal no more, yea let him work with his hands, that which is good so that he will have to give to those who need it." It has been my favorite verse in the Bible ever since that day, and I've read the Word many times. I can find no more profound statement. I would like to add that every word written in the Bible is profound and important, but that passage has directed my life since that day.

CHAPTER 11

GOOD AND EVIL
WITH POETRY

I worked at the steel mill for several years. This was the era before PLCs. We relied on relays and timing logic. Big, massive, high-inertia motors were what ran the rolling mills in those days. In a few years, I was made head of the maintenance department. When the boss gave me the title, he also gave me a dollar more per hour. I looked at him and demanded two more dollars per hour. I knew I was worth it, and I have had to fight for proper pay several times in my career. Employers won't give it up easily, but you must know your own worth and also that everyone is replaceable.

I had been baptized as a youth but felt the need to do it again. A coworker and his wife invited me to their church. We went every Sunday for five or six weeks. I accepted God's invite to the altar and pronounced, "Jesus is my Lord and Savior."

Then I took the plunge into baptism. I still hadn't read the Bible but now knew that I was like the seed that fell among thorns from the book of Matthew. The cares of this world choked the Word out of me.

I took a break after that last sentence, and the voices are telling me God is taking my house away from me. I say to them, "Godspeed in doing so. If God wants my house, then take it from me. He has something better in mind." In Psalms, like I said before, God says to be content with food and raiment. I say now to the voices one of my poems that I will include later on in this book. "I can sleep anywhere. Home is best, but all I need is a place to rest."

Let me add this: schizophrenia is different with everyone. Just like everyone is an individual, the lifestyles they've led custom-make their form of schizophrenia. No drug that was ever made, or ever will be made, can cure it. I take my medication every night around six o'clock. The only reason I take it is to get to sleep. Without it, I cannot fall asleep anymore, and if I forget to take it until around nine o'clock then I fall asleep three hours later. No medication does one bit of good in curing schizophrenia. I believe the medical profession seeks to help people with this disease and medication is a step in the healing process, but God has the only cure.

I believe in both good and evil. I am certain that good will triumph over evil. I can't really understand why anyone would want to do evil or even why there are evil spirits. Don't they know their efforts are futile? Hell holds a place for evil. Though evil may rejoice in the here and now, why does it exist if the end result is to burn in a lake of fire for time everlasting? I don't get it. You will never hear a lie come out of my mouth. I may not say everything that I should, but I cannot lie. Why should I? Why does anyone? I'm like Pastor Arnold Murray. He strikes me as a man willing to fight tooth and nail over anything with anyone when he believes he is doing God's will. I've listened to him many times, and I don't agree with everything he says, but I believe he thinks he is right. That's enough to respect him.

I'm no saint by any means. I find myself having little patience—mainly with my driving. The other day someone flipped me off at an intersection. I backed up, turned, and raced up to him while yelling out the window, "You got a problem with my driving?" Luckily he said, "No." I'm a big and intimidating man. Six feet tall and 220 pounds. I believe I helped that man avoid a future ass whopping by showing him the error of his ways. You don't go around flipping people off when they have done nothing against you. Maybe now he will think twice before he does it again.

I try not to let people get away with wrongdoing for just that reason, and I'm capable of fighting for it if I have to just to help them.

Anyway, I learned a lot from working with relays in the old steel mill. It was during this time I had been drinking heavily. My drink of choice was Jack Daniels with A & W Diet Cream Soda, a nasty combination. I had two beautiful dogs. I don't remember the breed, but they cost me two hundred dollars each. My mom was staying with me and she cooked nice meals. I couldn't eat anything for a couple of weeks and tossed my meals out the window to my dogs. I was so depressed with my girlfriend situation that I just drank all the time. It was hectic at work. We were converting the steel mill from the old-style logic to PLCs and DC drives. I was the head coordinator of the project. Sheffield Steel had bought the company and hired a crew from Chicago to do the changes. I took a trip to Chicago and got my first lesson on PLCs.

One day, in my confused state after not eating for a week or so and drinking heavily, I set up a chair in the backyard with my dogs. I took a notebook and spent a couple of hours in the sunshine writing some poems. I was mainly writing about my current situation in life. Here they are . . .

The problems I've had are the ones I've made. Can I pay them off? Can I get paid?

I've always wanted to live my life as in a shell. To hell with that. Let's party; let's raise some hell.

I wish I could write some happy rhymes, but my thoughts are filled with painful times.

I long to live for that place in time, where everything adheres to my sense of divine.

I thought my deeds were the key, yet everyone still underestimates me.

I purchase goods every day, but I sell myself in order to pay.

The oddest thing my life has seen is no matter how hard I try I can't recall my dreams.

People change, this is true. But no matter what, the one you love must accept you.

I question a friend. I receive a handshake. I look into his eyes and determine if he's fake.

Do other people feel the pain I know? So many hearts, I suppose so.

Am I rich or am I poor? Can you tell from my belongings? Are you sure?

Simple Sam, simple Dan. I think I am who I know I am.

Insecurity, is the definition clear? How I define it is pleasing a lover in fear.

I am who I am, but I can be who you are wanting to see.

I can sleep anywhere home is best, but all I need is a place to rest.
Happiness comes but once in a while very few things can make me smile.
I'm tired I'm lonely getting older everyday I'm wasting my time I don't want to play.
People come and people go how many of them do I really know.

What to do when things get to you.

Turn one way and scream and shout.

Turn the other way and throw things about.

Turn cold and let the wind blow.

Turn loose and let your cares go.

Turn on and give it all you got.

Turn off and give a care not.

Turn to the bottle and get yourself right.

Turn to drugs and say goodnight.

Turn to friends and see what begins.

Turn to family and maybe it will end.

Turn to the one for whom you yearn.

From all this sanity may be earned.

CHAPTER 12

TUCSON ROUND ONE

A couple of months later, it was time to move on. It just so happened, as I was alone in my empty rental house and crying over the loss of my current girlfriend, that my best friend called from Tucson. He and his new wife sensed my pain and told me to leave everything and come live with them.

I finished up the renovation of the plant and trained a couple of men to take my place. Then I put in my two-week notice. When time was up, I headed for what I thought was paradise. About a year before I left OKC, I was very drunk one night. I lived in a bad part of town and was at a convenience store. I must have badmouthed a big, black guy, because for some reason I said, "Come over to my apartment." It was a small, multifamily dwelling. Only three apartments and mine was in the center. I don't remember anything after that. I woke up to a phone call from my mom saying she was told in a dream by my great aunt, named Hope, that I was in danger. I could see myself in the headboard mirror of my bed and I looked like I had the hell beaten out of me. I told her not to worry and that all was fine. I quickly got off the phone. I walked to the convenience store where I knew the girl I was dating would be working. She closed the store and took me to the emergency room. A few days later, I had my four front teeth pulled. I went ten years without a partial denture. It didn't hurt my self-esteem too much. I still had many women in my life. I just avoided talking too much.

I moved to Tucson for the first of two times. About a week after being there, I had a job interview in Phoenix. I drove up there and went through the interview but could sense that it wasn't going to pan out, so I took the short trip to Laughlin, Nevada.

I was sitting at a blackjack table and in walked these two women. I was drinking, of course, so I blew one a kiss. She came over and sat down next to me. I gave her one hundred dollars' worth of chips, and she lost it all. So we went back to the motel she was staying at. I found out that she was traveling from New York City and trying to get to LA. She got stuck in Laughlin and was turning tricks to get by. After a wild evening with another couple, who I believed were married so I didn't have sex with the other woman, I told her I'd take her to LA. The next morning we dropped the married woman off at the welfare department and headed west.

We got there and looked around, walked down Hollywood Boulevard, stayed the night in a cheap hotel on Sunset Strip and then stayed one more night in another cheap hotel near downtown LA. This one had porn on the TV, and she asked me to tie her up like what was on the screen. I said, "Sorry, I don't have rope." She said. "Use your shoestrings." So we had some fun and then decided to head to Phoenix to look for work.

She was very beautiful and said she could easily get a job in a strip joint in Phoenix while I sought employment. I rented a motel for a week. Three days later, I called my buddy in Tucson and let him know what was going on. He said to forget her and get back to Tucson. I gave her some story and left her a silver spoon from my silverware set I had in the trunk and told her I would be back for it. I never returned. I saw her about nine months later back in Laughlin. I didn't approach her. I ducked into a casino until she passed by. She left a roll of film in my car from her travels from New York. I never developed it. Maybe someday I'll dig it out of the box where I keep what few possessions I managed to retain and have it developed.

I stayed with my buddy for a short while then got a job with a temp company and rented my own apartment. I did some odd jobs for about six months then went to a bookstore and read the want ads. An obscure plant in a remote town of eastern Texas was looking for an industrial electrical maintenance technician. I decided I would drive the long trip and stay one night in a motel and let the company know I needed the decision about getting hired by tomorrow, or I was leaving for Oklahoma. I was flat broke and had just enough gas money to get back to my mom.

CHAPTER 13

CORRIGAN TEXAS

One of the workers called my motel around 11:30, right before I was heading out, and gave me the job. I accepted the job and started the next day. This was a great time to be an industrial electrical maintenance technician. This plant made plywood. A lot of precision equipment was involved, and the company had the latest computers. I think they ran on DOS 2.0. The company had Allen Bradley PLCs—the best you can use.

I spent many hours with a coworker named Paul Ted Adams. He and I worked the night shift, and we definitely were smarter than the rest of the crew combined. We would analyze everything in the plant unencumbered, and we did our jobs well. He became an electrical engineer. Corrigan was located in the Piney Woods. Lots of rain and the clouds were always grey. I got depressed quite often and looked for ways to entertain myself. I would often practice my golf, pitching wedge shots in an old unused baseball park just outside the facility. It caught on and soon people were joining me. We had a little campsite next to some trees by the ballpark. A bunch of us would cook out and hit golf shots in the early morning. Lots of ice cold beer to go along with the Texas barbeques. I learned how to play craps and dominoes fairly well.

I did some computer work for my rich landlord. He bought up loans from Kirby Vacuum Sales and made a fortune. He gave me as a gift one of the first PCs ever made. It was a dealer's unit and had many "basic" language programs. Ted and I hacked them every morning we got off work when we were not playing golf. We would take the programs apart front and back and re-write them. Most of the time they ended up much better than the design of the initial programmer. I gave it to another coworker who couldn't afford a new computer and wish I had saved it. It was something!

I fell into the wrong crowd at that time. I met this black girl who was addicted to crack cocaine. She got me hooked on it, and I was living paycheck to paycheck. She found my checkbook and wrote many hot checks. At the local supermarket, there was a sign as you walk in: "Do not accept Checks from 'Ray Edgell.'" I was shocked, so I went to the counter. Sure enough, the store had about ten checks with my forged signature. I had to go to the police station and file a report on the bogus checks, and then I went through a long legal battle over them.

My addiction got pretty bad, and I lost my job. My mom and sister came to save me. They made the six-hour trip and talked me into leaving. I cashed in an old insurance policy from my National Guard days and paid off my truck that I had bought from my landlord. He didn't believe me when I told him I would pay it off in three or four days. I was never one to lie and was shocked at his disbelief. I paid him and we kept in contact. About a year later my landlord and his wife called me to come back and work on their computer systems again. He said he would give me a twenty-five-horsepower motor for the boat I had in Oklahoma. I made the trip and stayed the night. I guess they were swingers. They gave me a porno movie to watch, and I never caught on because I was still pretty naive in that regard. But I didn't join them in bed, even though she came into the room wearing nothing but a smile. Something inside me said, "No," to adultery. I was very tempted and almost gave in, but I didn't do it.

CHAPTER 14

HOME AGAIN

Well, I was back in Altus. I was about thirty-three or thirty-four years old by this time. I took a job with Bar-S foods as an electrical maintenance technician. I was clean from drugs for a good while and passed the drug screen to get hired. Electrical maintenance is a great job, if you can get it. Lots of free time. When something goes wrong it usually takes a minute or two to fix and you are a hero. Once Bill Lay, my supervisor and I were given the task to figure out the problem with the plant managers' computer system. The IT guy had told the manager there must be some kind of wiring problem from his computer to the server. I didn't think so but Bill and I checked it out. This took about an hour. We could find nothing wrong and Bill said "let's start over", while scratching his head. I said let me have a look at his computer. I hit the F12 button upon startup and went into the CMOS section. I noticed that communications was set to com port 1 when it should have been on com port 2. I changed the setting and he was in business. If I had been alone I would have fixed it in five minutes but I had to listen to my boss. We got a nice letter of accommodation from my supervisors' supervisor and I still have the letter. I know a college degree is an exceptional thing to have, but for those who don't want to continue their education in that manner I recommend entering technical college. Years later, back in Tucson for the second time, my nephew came to live with me. Steven Ray didn't graduate high school so I immediately suggested getting his GED. He got it in about two months. I told him my path in life began with technical college, and he enrolled. Today he is highly successful and has a great and secure job with a lifetime skill. He also has his own side business doing some form of computer work. His instructor later came to work with me at Avent, Kimberly Clark. A company I worked for at that time in Tucson. I guess I had worked for Bar-S in Altus for about nine months, and it was okay. I could do the job in my sleep, so there wasn't much challenge for me. Bill and I would often go fishing in small ponds and sometimes at the lake. The lake has a large dam. One spring the lake was full and they were releasing water from the dam. Bill and I, without fear, got into the raging river at the low-water crossing and tried to fish. We must have been crazy. We were up to our necks in rushing water. I look back on it and can't believe we did that. One slip and we would have certainly drowned.

My buddy, Bryon, called me again from Tucson. He said he had just completed a training course for golf-club making and repairs. He asked if I wanted to be his partner. I could live with his family again rent free, he would pay my expenses, and I could golf all day in the beautiful weather of Tucson. He made it sound so good that I immediately went to human resources at Bar-S and gave my termination notice. An HR employee offered me two more dollars per hour on the spot. I said to him, "Thanks, but I'd rather be golfing!" So I headed out on another journey into the unknown.

It was the best time of my life.

CHAPTER 15

BACK TO TUCSON

Now I want to begin writing down the things that I believe brought on schizophrenia. None of the three doctors that diagnosed me could tell me why I got the disease. I will also describe in detail the onset of the disease. I still have family living around me and will be as exact and to the point as I can, without full disclosure of a few details. I don't feel it was any one thing that brought it on. I feel it was a culmination of the many acts during my entire life, with emphasis on this period.

This journey began in 1995. I had a Ford Ranger pickup and was able to haul a few possessions to Tucson with me. I arrived at my good friend Bryon's house and greeted his wife and newborn son. They had a five-year-old daughter and a middle son as well. I moved in and got comfortable, and soon we opened a shop doing golf-club repair at a driving range on the other side of Tucson. It was the most enjoyable job I ever had.

We would begin the morning by checking in at a sporting-goods store called Play It Again Sports. We would do its entire club repairs, which generally took from a half hour to an hour and a half. Then we went to our little club repair shop at the driving range.

We had lots of downtime. We spent way too much time on the driving range. The manager let us hit balls for free. I got pretty good—about a twelve handicap—and my buddy, who I never could beat, was about a five handicap. We would often close up shop and go golfing, at least twice a week.

One weekend the driving range held a million-dollar hole-in-one contest. We didn't have a putting green, but workers added one the week before the event. I only practiced on it once or twice. I entered the putting contest. They set the hole twenty feet away, and contestants bought one ball for a dollar; I think we got two free if we bought five. Bryon and I had very little money, and our whole enterprise was staked by his wife, who was a court clerk for a district judge. I managed to buy fourteen balls. I made two of the putts and went to the finals. I was number eight in line out of the nine people who had made at least one putt. The first seven went through, and no one hit the cup.

It came to my turn, and I sank the first putt. And then I putted my second ball to three quarters of an inch away from the hole. The ninth and final guy putted, and I was sure he was going to make it, but his stopped a half inch from the hole. So I won, and then the directors had a discussion for who would get the third-place prize. One of the directors said I should get it, and he asked me for my feelings on the matter. I said, "Sure, why not?" I won the prize money and also got a Ping Budweiser golf bag, three head covers for the woods, and a Budweiser Ray Cook putter. I was very proud of myself and told my girlfriend, who was a stripper. She would often come to the driving range for lessons, which is how we met—not at a strip joint, although I visited her there several times!

Someone spoke up that my victory was tainted because I worked there. I tried to explain that the green was just put in and I had no experience with it so the directors let me have the prizes. One guy followed me to the repair shop and offered to buy the bag, head covers, and putter. I think I sold them all for a small amount like a hundred dollars. I was on top of the world, and as I was driving home I took the exit to the greyhound track to place a bet on the trifecta. I won it also.

I went home and told Bryon and he was shocked. We would often play a putting game called seven-up at other driving ranges and golf courses. We did this at least a hundred times. I never once beat him. So naturally I had to brag on winning and placing third in a citywide event. Tucson is a big city, so it was a big victory! He couldn't claim any victories better than that.

When we were fourteen or fifteen back in Altus, he and I were on a bowling team together. One week we got published in a nationwide magazine for having the second-highest series as a team in the country. He always had about a fifteen- to twenty-pin higher average than I had. We were sitting in a local taco joint about a week before the state tournament in Tulsa, and I said I was going to take high series scratch. He said that if I did that by beating him along with all the other contestants in the state, he would go out on Main Street and drop his pants and crap a turd then put a flag in it and sing "The Star-Spangled Banner." He never made good on the promise.

I also won all events with handicap. In Tucson and the surrounding suburbs, golf courses would frequently hold little tournaments. One weekend Bryon and I, with a friend I called Double D—for Dissing Dave, because he would often make a date to go with us and blow us off by not showing up. He was married; that was his excuse. The three of us went to a tournament in a suburb, and we just knew we had the right chemistry that day. You could win money by getting the low score for each hole, if no other team matched it. We won the third hole. Dave hit an incredible drive, it was a best-ball format, and Bryon hit a pretty good second shot. It was a long par five. His ball ended up thirty feet from the hole. I said, "I got this. Let me putt first." I sank it. We also won another hole on a spectacular iron shot I made to within four feet of the cup. It was on a slope so we raced up there to mark it before it rolled down. It came down to the last hole: a par three. Our best ball from the tee was about four feet below the fringe. We were one shot behind the leading team. It was make or lose. We had to chip in. Both Bryon and Dave missed. I took aim and made a perfect shot and drained it. Officials held a putt-off to see who got the first-place prize money, and I didn't come through, as I was sure I would.

We finished second. At least during the play of golf we had beaten all the teams and tied the eventual winner.

We struggled making clubs for about a year and a half then his wife pulled the plug. I was at the house one day about a month after she took away our fun times waiting on a phone call from a potential employer. The phone rang. Everyone else was gone, so I answered. It was a man calling for Bryon's wife. I could sense something was up and told Bryon. We never had a physical fight in our lives, but I shut my mouth quick after his demeanor changed.

A few weeks later, reality sat in and I had to move out. So did Bryon. His wife rented him an apartment. His wife's dad came over and made it clear to Bryon not to cause any problems, and he threatened me with having made sexual advances to Bryon's little girl. I think she was seven at the time. Sex is a predominant thought in every man's life, but I learned early on to differentiate fantasy and acts that could get you killed or put in prison. I was speechless when he said that and simply moved out.

CHAPTER 16

WORLD TRAVELER

It just so happened that I had, at this time, completed my third interview with the company I was trying to get hired on with: Avent. I thought it was just a little company that made textiles. After working there about three months, I found out it had recently been acquired by Kimberly Clark, a *Fortune 500* company.

This plant had seven high-speed diameter-compensating reels that would unwind large rolls of various fabrics and allow you to lay them on a very large table where you could then use automatic knives to cut out patterns. It sounds like a simple operation, but you must consider the waste factor. And that is where the logic for *compensation* comes in.

The reels had opto modules controlling the logic and a computer interface. Not a very good system. Before I was hired, employees would have the company that built them come for service calls and do repairs. I was familiar with the opto systems and ended all that. I saved Avent a bunch of cash. This was when NAFTA was in full swing. An engineer with Kimberly Clark proposed a change to the logic of these systems. I had heard that they were preparing to move all the machines to various countries, mainly Mexico. He came up with the initial design and then left the company to become a monk in Colorado.

My boss asked me if I could take over and implement these changes. I was very familiar with PLCs and used the mathematical straight-line equation formula to calibrate the reels. I had never used this type of PLC but said, "I'll have the first one done in a week, if you relieve me from my other duties."

I designed the initial layout of the physical inputs and outputs and the processor. I then loaded the program on the first reel. It was a success. We ran it a month or so in our facility to tweak the program. I was the programmer and installer of the equipment and soon found out I would be the one tearing it down and packing it into a shipping container, a semi-truck, and reinstalling it in foreign countries. George, my boss, had already taken me down to get a passport, and the day I got it we did our first trip into Mexico.

We flew to a place called Guaymus, where our plant had a very old PLC that was user-*unfriendly*. It took me about ten minutes to master it, and we solved its issues and went sightseeing.

I liked traveling to foreign destinations and doing easy—that is, easy for me—work. The best part is the work only took a short period of time, and I got to enjoy the places I visited.

My boss loved beer as much as I did, and we spent lots of time just driving around while looking at the sites with an ice chest full of the local beers. He was much older and wasn't interested in the women too much.

This first place, Guaymus, was a big town on the Pacific coast of Mexico near the resort town of San Carlos. We stayed in a hotel overlooking a bay with lots of ships docked. The hotel had a quaint bar and the people were so full of life. I was hooked. I had an expense account and a corporate credit card. I had to fill out expense reports but never once was questioned about my expenditures.

In my seven-year career with Kimberly Clark, I went to Mexico about five hundred times. We had two plants in Nogales about a sixty-mile drive from Tucson, one in Magdalena, two in Guaymus, and one in the central part of Mexico near Mexico City. We had one plant in Honduras, one in Slovakia, and one in China. I racked up the frequent-flyer miles.

I felt that I had made the corporation lots of money and wasn't being paid right for what I did. I asked for a raise. When nothing happened for a week, I gave them my two-week notice and got hired on at a plant making catheters. I actually was working both jobs at the same time, because Kimberly Clark waited until I was walking out to give me a two-dollar-an-hour raise. Of course I stayed. I liked the traveling. About a week later, my bosses promoted me to a new position within the engineering department and gave me a raise of a little more than two more dollars per hour. My first office job.

I did little in the office. I just browsed the Internet sites and did a lot of stock trading. I had several women in every town that I worked in. Two of the people who would often travel with me had wives, and they cheated on them every chance they got. I said within myself it was wrong, but I was happy to have company for the nightlife.

One married engineer who traveled with me a lot to Honduras had dated this girl who now lives in New York. Her name is Emmy. She introduced me to a young woman who was just fourteen. I wasn't sure if I should be with her, but it was Honduras. I visited her mom to get the okay. Her mom was younger than I was. Anyway, I was there for a two-week period that had a one-week Easter break in the middle. I asked my boss if I could take a week's vacation and he said, "Sure." So I rented a room at a bed-and-breakfast on the island of Roatan.

The young girl, Ligia, wanted to stay with me, and with her mom's okay we took a hop over to the island. This was my second visit to the island. It just so happened that the owners of the small hotel had made a booking error, and we were the only guests. Ligia and I took a boat cruise over to a small, deserted island that was no larger than a football field and spent the day snorkeling and making out on the isolated beach. Then back at the hotel we were having sex again, and she didn't want me to pull out. I found out she wanted to get pregnant. I would have none of that, and she got angry.

I left Honduras but came back about a month later. Emmy said Ligia had been going to one of the hotels we had stayed at and was having sex with people there. I guess she just wanted a baby. Emmy was dismayed that the other engineer had left her. She had been dating one of the married engineers that often accompanied me on my journeys. So Emmy and I started dating. She was more my age. For some reason, she wanted to keep it a secret. She may have had her reasons, but I wasn't happy about it.

A group of us, on the company credit card, went to a local nightspot. She wanted to keep it a secret so I, feeling bad about it, thought I would help her out by hitting on the cocktail server. I gave her the address and room number of the hotel and said for her to come by after her shift. That got Emmy to thinking, and boy was she mad!

CHAPTER 17

SEPTEMBER 11TH 2001

At this point in my life, I was ready to settle down and get married. On September 10, 2001, I closed on a house in Tucson. My first home. I had the movers scheduled to come over the morning of the eleventh. I woke up ready to make the move. I had taken the day off, so I wasn't at work when the planes started the attack. I watched the events unfold live on TV and was as shocked as everyone else was. The movers still showed up. I went ahead as scheduled and unlocked the door to my new home.

A part of me feels some demon spirits from the tragedies of the day moved in with me. I had a home computer and really got into the pornography found on the Internet. I have a very addictive nature, so I was hooked. I would spend hours after work drinking Jack Daniels mixed with diet soda while watching porn. I really needed to find a wife.

I thought of Emmy. I had tried to get her to move to Tucson from Honduras, but I found out she was still married to someone in New York and had to go there. I'm pretty sure this is one of the times I committed adultery. I had to go back to Honduras, and Emmy set up a lunch date to meet her parents. After dinner, I took them to my room to call Emmy. The connection wasn't too good, but I could perceive that she wasn't going to be my wife.

The next day at the plant, I met the woman of my dreams, Alba Luz Ramirez Chavez. She was a seamstress. I asked her out, and within a week I asked if she would like to get married. Before she answered, she asked me about Jesus. I said, "Mejor en mi corazon." First in my heart. She went to the church every day to pray. I asked her to lunch the first day and she said yes. I took her shopping and bought her and her girlfriend some clothes in the mall in San Pedro Sula. That store in the mall was a very expensive place to get clothes. It was twice the amount for similar clothes back home. We then went to the luxury hotel my company had got me for the two weeks stay.

Her girlfriend lay on the bed the whole time. I knew nothing was going to happen and was inwardly glad. I spent about ten minutes brushing Alba's hair while looking at her in the mirror. Certainly one of the best ten-minute periods of my life. It was then that I told her I wanted to get married. I didn't say married *to her*, but she took it as so and agreed. I said, "I can't wait to get married so I can have you." She coyly said, "I'm not a virgin." I think she was twenty-one and I wasn't disappointed at the news, but I was going to wait with her until we did get married. I loved her that much!

We never got married. I should have done it that day, but the next day I had to leave and wouldn't be back for some time. Little did I realize that I never would be back? It is the greatest tragedy of my life, surpassing even this disease. The voices say all this happened to bring me home to my family. Daily they say, "We're sending you back to . . ." and I fill in the blank of Honduras.

I had a little day fling with the hotel maid and came back home. That's when all hell broke loose in my life.

CHAPTER 18

THE DIAGNOSIS

I need to get into the meat of the matter dealing with what I believe was the main reason I got the disease. First, I want to talk about the last eight years, since I was forced to move home, and how my life is today. This may give you some idea of how to battle this disease.

I was crippled literally when I came home. I had a broken heel of my right foot from jumping off a Tucson overpass to retrieve a crack pipe I had tossed into a field outside my hotel.

I was crippled spiritually and physically. I knew I wasn't crazy but had been devastated from the events that I will describe further as you read.

I couldn't drive the U-Haul on this twelve-hour trip from Tucson to come home to my mom, so I convinced the girl who was living with me in Tucson to drive me. She was like a sister to me, and when I asked, she did say she loved me—even though we never had sex. She witnessed a lot of the devastation. I spent eight hundred dollars on the U-Haul and had very few possessions left. It was a big waste; the U-Haul was three quarters empty. I don't feel God wanted me to bring anything with me, but I was stubborn.

We moved into my mom's house, where I currently reside. She was only fifty-four at the time. She was married to a nice, young, black man who, although religious, had been having affairs. It devastated my mom. God surely brought me home to be with my family. He was a supervisor at Bar-S, but my mom's rants at the facility forced him to quit. She was viciously jealous, and she had good reason to be mad at him. He was younger than me by a couple of years. I knew it wouldn't work. He took the law-enforcement test and became a cop in a small town about thirty-five miles away to get away from her. They are still legally married.

I sent the girl, whose name I can't remember, back to Tucson on a bus. It is strange but I can't remember any names of the acquaintances I had in Tucson during the last year there. I got a job with Bar-S for the second time. The voices had just really started to get bad, and I tried to maintain and work hard, but the elevated noise level of the nitrogen air-conditioning system in the plant combined with the blowers was too much. The voices use any type of machine noise to talk over or through. They still use these means. As I sit here writing this, I can hear them talking to me over the fan blowing on me. Another trick they used in Tucson a few times, they employed again. They would talk over the car radio as if it were a ten-minute infomercial. They were trying to get me to look for a place in northern California where the voices can't penetrate. It was like a talk show dealing with schizophrenia. The people on the show never used the word *schizophrenia*; they just talked about voices in their heads. The guest was describing that this was the only place he could get away from the voices.

Putting two and two together, I should have remembered this because they tried to get me to go back to Honduras a few weeks later. I believe they were just messing with me to take all my money and place me in a desperate situation.

I started working for Bar-S again and it only lasted three months. I couldn't take the noise level that was enveloped with the never ending screaming from the voices. I went to the Human Resources lady and said I can't take it anymore. Bar-S placed me on a one-year medical leave, which became indefinite. The doctor the Human Resources lady sent me to diagnosed me with paranoid schizophrenia. That was the first time I heard the term schizophrenia used. I had no idea of what this disease was. He deduced this from a written test that I feel I aced; it was more like an IQ test. We had a lengthy discussion in which I described to him what I felt the government was doing to me.

At this time, I was out of work and trusted my mother with opening a joint account at her bank. I deposited about $25,000 from my cashed-out 401(k) plan. The voices were constantly bombarding me, and I turned to the pipe for a while because I was still addicted to cocaine—I just wasn't using while working at Bar-S. I didn't do much and spent very little of my money on it. I haven't done any crack in many years. I even quit drinking. It's been at least two years since I drank any form of alcohol.

My Aunt Veda died during this time. I had thousands of frequent-flyer miles, so I sent everyone to the state of Washington to be with her. She had six children. My mom also used one ticket. I surmised that she took money from our account and bought another ticket to Seattle to meet some guy she had met on the Internet. I don't know what all she was buying, but a month or so later my $25,000 was gone. I think she bought extra flights, etc. I don't know for sure, but one day I suggested ordering pizza and she said the money was gone.

She's had a tough life. I know of a few times she attempted suicide. The last time this occurred, she was at our home and distraught over Willy, I believe. She just staggered in and was incoherent. I decided not to call the paramedics, because they would send her to an institution for a long while and she was a smoker. It would be very difficult on her. I finally got her comfortably in bed and spent some time praying for her. I checked her breathing and watched her for a few hours. She made it through the night.

She told me the next morning she had taken all her pills. She informed me, "I'm gonna give you this house." A few months later, she and Willy signed over the title. Then she gave me her car, which used to be my grandma's. I felt it was a nice trade; I needed a home and car but not that money.

I did a lot of fishing during this period. There were no machinery noises, so the voices were quieter but still intense. It was a little respite, but you can't imagine the intensity level during these days, weeks, and months. I went fishing often to escape to a degree. I had applied for unemployment insurance from Bar-S. I was denied, because the unemployment office couldn't locate my wages. After many attempts to get the insurance, I noticed they had the wrong social security number. The voices so disrupted me when I got hired on at Bar-S the second time that I wrote down the wrong social security number on my paperwork.

CHAPTER 19

MY ATTEMPTED SUICIDE

I was dead broke for only the second time in my life. I had only gone hungry one day in my life. This was while living in Corrigan after I lost the job at the plywood factory. Graciously an old couple that lived nearby gave me one meal and the old gentleman wrote down his thoughts along with some Scripture. I still have the letter in my portfolio of achievements and important documents. They saved my life and I sold them my personal computer to have gas money to get home.

I was fishing in a quiet spot at the reservoir near to my home, and I believe the Holy Spirit said to me, "Apply for social security." I didn't know you could get it under the age of 62 for any reason, but I immediately left off fishing and raced home and applied online. I suffered for about eight more months with no unemployment benefits. I was desperately waiting for the judgment from the social security administration. I've heard that 75 percent of the people who apply get denied, but I had three doctors who were treating or had treated me for this disease, and my mom wrote a nice accompanying letter. The social security administration required it from someone who knew you.

About seven and a half months before I got the notification of the impending monthly disbursement, the voices ultimately got to me. It was a cold day, and I think that was the only reason I didn't drive my brother-in-law's car into the reservoir to drown myself. I didn't like the thought of freezing and drowning to death. I told the voices to quit now or I was going to overdose. They intensified.

My psychologist had prescribed some powerful sleeping pills, and I took about fifty to sixty of them and then lay down.

Something came over me and said, "Go throw them up." I went to the back porch and tried but couldn't. I went to my mom's bedroom and told her I had a problem and needed her, but she was on the phone with Willy. In her state of mind, she didn't want to stop talking. I went back to my room and lay down again.

I got real frightened. I was starting to feel sleep coming on and forced myself up one last time. I opened her door again and said I overdosed and needed to get to the hospital.

She raced me to the hospital that wasn't very far away, and medical professionals pumped my stomach. They said I died and I didn't come out of it for about twenty-six hours.

When I woke up, there were tubes in all my cavities and my dad and mom were sitting at my bedside. My dad had driven from Houston, which was a twelve to thirteen-hour trip, and he said he had been there a while. I knew I had lost some time. The police then transported me to a mental institution.

I hadn't done many drugs during this time, or even when I was working at Bar-S, which drug-screened everyone. I was clean. I had done quite a bit in Tucson, but it was mostly social. I've heard that drugs are a major cause of schizophrenia, but I'm not sure. I believe it is a culmination of a lifestyle and doing drugs is a part of it, but that's not the sole reason one acquires it. The Gospels talk of many people possessed with demon spirits. They certainly didn't have the drugs we have today. Reach any conclusion you want about the cause of this disease, but in my life, as you may determine, I don't feel drugs had a major part in it. Addiction maybe. God tries to correct his children. I am currently addicted to about seven things: my art collection, smoking, reading the Bible, pain pills, cookie dough, coffee, and driving too quickly. I'm working on all of them except the smoking and Bible reading.

A few years back, I tried to quit smoking. I went thirteen days without a smoke. The voices had quieted down a bit, and I thought it would work out fine. I couldn't take going without the smoke while the voices kept talking in my head. I bought one pack. I made a heartfelt statement to God and to the voices, saying, "I will only try to quit once the voices leave me."

For some reason, there is an antismoking campaign. Sure, it bothers your breathing, but as far as it killing you, I don't buy it. Picasso lived until his nineties. He was a chain smoker. I believe wholeheartedly that God has the date of your death marked in time. Nothing can change that date. Quality of life can be, and is, changed from smoking. So for health reasons, I understand the campaign against smoking, but don't tell me it kills you!

I mentioned that the voices had tried to get me to take a trip back to Honduras to get Alba Luz Ramirez Chavez, who is the love of my life and second only to Jesus. I love my mom a lot, but the Bible says in a couple of places, "for this cause shall a man leave his parents to be joined in marriage". I'll clue you in. The Holy Trinity should be loved first, then your spouse and yourself as you are joined together, and then everyone else. My mom, dad, and sisters along with children should get the same love as perhaps any friend or foe.

Think about it. The Bible talks about brotherly love being very important. When told by his disciples that his mother and other family members wanted to see him, Jesus said in Matthew Ch.12 vs. 50, "For whosoever shall do the will of my Father which is in Heaven the same is my mother brothers and sisters." Jesus also says in many places in the Bible to love your neighbor as yourself. Love your enemies and do good unto them that despise you. I love my mother with all my heart, but no more than the person who lives on the next block.

Love is simple to understand by reading God's Word. Life is just a big test. It's very similar to those tests from your school days. I feel God will grade you on Judgment Day. If you pass, he will say, "Well done, my good and faithful servant. Enter into thine reward." You were given grades like A, B, C, D, and F in school, and in most cases those grades determined what your future career would be. I believe God will bless those who bless others in this life and will reward them openly now and in heaven.

CHAPTER 20

TRYING TO REACH ALBA

I was sitting at home in Altus; the nearest airport is sixty-five miles away. I don't remember how I got there. It could very well be I was transported there by the Spirit. I just don't recall. I went into the airport, and the voices told me to go to the electronic machine that issued tickets and to type in the code, and then I would be on my way to Honduras. To Alba.

The voices started reciting the numbers to me, and I was typing them in. The numbers never produced a ticket. I tried for hours. I then walked out of the airport and had no transportation. I still had the broken heel, but as painful as it was I started walking to the highway. I was going to hitch a ride home.

I was confused, and the voices were magnified. They told me to close my eyes and walk a straight line in the middle of the feeder road. I walked for miles this way. I then went back to the airport and tried the machine again. The airport was closing; there would be no more flights. The voices said to go to OKC to catch a flight.

I started walking down the highway to locate a motel. I was near a motel when a bird in a tree started talking to me. It was the same jibber-jabber the voices had been saying all day. Dogs had talked to me in Tucson, so, although amazing, I got over the surprise of having a blackbird talk to me.

I was in a lot of pain and struggled to get to the first motel. The desk clerk denied me a room, so I struggled down the highway and eventually caught a cab and drove back to the airport for some reason.

It was dark, and the airport was closed. I took off on foot again and reached another motel. That desk clerk also denied me. I knew where the bus depot was and limped there. I waited on the morning bus to OKC.

I slept a little in the rain and caught a bus to OKC the next morning. I got dropped off at its airport.

I was in agony but felt if I could just get the ticket and get on the plane to Honduras, then all would be fine. The voices played the same game, but this time there were two ticket machines: one upstairs and one downstairs. I must have made ten or more trips in agony up and down the stairs while trying to get the correct code for the machine to spit out the ticket. Finally, I was stopped by a security guard who told me to leave or he would place me under arrest. I tried to explain, but how could I?

I left and got a motel. The next day, I took the bus back to Lawton and called my cousin, Danny. He drove the sixty miles to pick me up at the bus station. That was a hideous game the voices had played on me. Later in Altus, they tried to get me to drive with my eyes closed. I tried it for a while then realized the game they were playing was the same as at the airports. They seemed to want me arrested for what would seem to be mental problems or to have an accident.

Evidently, I had been pretty paranoid while in Tucson, but I didn't think so. I determined in my mind that the voices were a new, secret, government weapon, and I was one of the first guinea pigs. It wasn't until about a year after being home in Altus that I realized it was not the government but spirits. I would always hear helicopters hovering over me in Tucson. I would look into the night sky to see them, and I would see a point of light and focus on it, thinking it was a police helicopter surveying me from the distance. I felt strongly that this was taking place because once in Tucson a helicopter materialized from a point of light that I had been staring at for a while from a long distance. It flew directly over my house at a pretty low altitude.

CHAPTER 21

PARANOIA

I lived near the airport in Tucson. Either I heard it, or the voices planted the thought that police crime units have high-tech devices in big cities that can watch anyone from a long distance. They appear as a star in the night sky. I was amazed and stupefied by the way the government, as I perceived it, was using light. It would move metal objects into patterns and create force fields. It seemed they needed magnetism to do things like make me feel ill or take away my money and drugs. The government would use the lights, any lights, and intensify them to gather or move into an array of various metal objects.

I pointed this out to one of the women I was using drugs with one night. I was sitting on her couch and could feel powerful vibrations all around me. I told her the government was harassing me. I wasn't really sure who it was, but someone was building up a force field around me. I was so sure of it that I lifted up her couch. Directly under where I was sitting were six or seven household metal objects and tools of hers organized in a perfect circle? She looked at it but didn't even comment. I thought for sure she was a government plant, or perhaps was a spirit or an angel.

This paranoia was still very strong in Altus. When I had made a return trip to Tucson to get my car, I heard some old friends asking the girl that drove me, "Did he make it there undetected?" I saw their lips moving and heard those words, but stranger things have happened. I think the voices were up to tricks. A few times, people were sleeping and made threatening statements to me. This definitely happened at least twice. Once, one of my cousins was in the bedroom at my sister's house. I was awake and could hear him talking in his sleep, saying he was going to kick my ass. It was his voice, and the dialogue lasted a couple minutes. I was thinking about what he was saying, and my thoughts produced a nonverbal response that he would answer. I asked him about it a couple of days later, and he said he didn't know what I was talking about. It seemed the voices wanted me to get in to a confrontation with him for some reason.

I had never realized what a paranoid schizophrenic was until the doctor diagnosed me as such. I dismissed the paranoia part because it wasn't in my mind at all. All these things actually happened. Just like in the movie *A Brilliant Mind*, where the lead character saw the same group of people throughout his life. I have been hearing the same group of voices for eight years. I did see some people that were not there a few times. I'll talk about those when I describe the events of the final year in Tucson.

CHAPTER 22

TALKING TO GOD AND A LEAP OF FAITH

It was about this time when I began reading the Bible every day. I had never read it in its entirety, just a few passages now and then. I went to the church I had attended when I lived in the southern part of Altus as a youth. It was a Baptist church. If anyone asks, I'll call myself a Baptist, but denomination isn't the key factor in one's faith. It is believing in Jesus. I'm a Baptist.

I soaked in my pastor's words that I know were inspired by God. I left services one day and was halfway home before turning around. I went back and spoke to the preacher. I said I would like to become a member. I told him I had been baptized in this church as a youth and once again in a church in OKC as an adult. He welcomed me, and I went every

Sunday for a year or so. I still attend to this day, but I do miss a few Sundays now and then.

I started putting money in the plate and knew it was the right thing to do because churches give to those who need it. They help out the community God's way, and I couldn't do better than God's way. So every extra dime I had went to the church.

Very soon after this, I called the social security administration to inquire about my case. A woman over the phone said, "Congratulations. You get fifteen hundred plus per month." I was ecstatic. I was staying with my sister now because my mom knew how fragile I was after the suicide attempt, and she had her own problems with Willy. This was a few weeks after my attempted suicide.

As soon as I hung up the phone with the social security agency, my mom drove up and said my unemployment compensation had been granted. She handed me four or five weeks' worth of checks. I joyfully bought four or five pizzas, and we had a feast that night.

This is when I religiously started giving 10 percent of my income to the church to do God's will. A couple of months later, my sister died from sepsis. I had taken her to see a doctor a few days before she died. She wouldn't let me take her to the hospital, where the doctor encouraged her to go. I wasn't in the room with them, but I should have been. I didn't realize he had told her to get to a hospital. I found out months later. I took her home and made her some iced tea. She loved that tea. She hadn't had any in a long while and it was the dead of summer. It was like I had given her the best thing in the world at the time.

Willy was gone by now, and I moved back in with my mom to help support her in the house she had just signed over to me. The change of ownership occurred after I began going to church and tithing. Same thing with the car. The voices are ever present except when I am in church. They leave me alone completely there.

They also leave me alone while I'm league bowling. I did this for four years. It's a lot of fun. I once scored a 278. I once made eleven strikes out of twelve, almost a perfect game. I've never rolled a perfect game or had a hole-in-one at golf. I've come very close and am satisfied to have been physically able to play. I stopped bowling because there were too many times I would hit the pocket dead flush and not get a strike. I felt the voices or controlling spirits were manipulating the pins to enjoy my frustration.

I question myself with the little ability I have to form rational thoughts without the voices confusing them. To ask the voices is pointless. I can't believe anything they say anyway, so why even ask?

Has God forsaken me with this disease? Am I in hell now? Am I going to hell when I leave this physical body? I could very well now be condemned to an eternity in hell yet still be walking around.

My heart and the promises of the Bible tell me I'm going to heaven. The Bible says the hosts of heaven rejoice over one sinner who repents. For the last eight or nine years, I've tried so hard to do just and good things for everyone in need. I picked up a wallet in a 7-Eleven and didn't even open it up. I handed it over to the counterperson. The next day I asked if she found the owner, and she said yes. She also said he was frantic, saying it had over three hundred dollars in it. I'll probably see him in heaven when we get there.

I had been giving 10 percent of my social security to the church for a few years. You wouldn't believe the blessings God poured out on me. I heard Pastor Murray from the Shepherds Chapel say, "If you're on a fixed income, don't worry about giving 10 percent to the church. Give what you can." So now I place some money on the plate every Sunday and help out friends and family as much as I can. I still get many blessings on a daily basis that I can't contain, but it's not like before when I was giving 10 percent. I have a few automatic deductions from my checking account to places like St. Jude's Children's Hospital and Childfund.org. The feelings I get when I see pictures and receive letters from the children that I help support are so great. I often cry when I receive them.

I don't want you to think I glory in my giving. To God be the glory. What I wish for you to understand is that it's true that the more you give, the more you receive. I wish I had known this when I was younger. I'd be a multimillionaire by now. Not that I would ever keep millions of dollars. I'd bless others with most of it. As the good book says, be content with food and raiment.

With me now are only two voices. I feel one is telling partial truths and the other is flat-out lying and saying opposing words to the other one. They sound alike, so I can't determine which is doing the lying. When it was really bad, there seemed to be about seven voices in my head.

I believe schizophrenia is different for everyone. I mean, there are billions of individuals in this world, and they are leading different lives. I think the disease is tailor-made to the individual. I've heard that God will not put on someone more than he can handle. I haven't read those exact words in the Bible though, and I did try to commit suicide. I was told

I died for a short period, but I didn't see any light or anything like it.

A few months after I attempted suicide, I was in bed and the voices told me my sister, who had passed away a year before, wanted to talk to me. She was in her thirties when she died. It was a very weak connection to her and I didn't make out much. I can't remember any part of the conversation. I lay back down when I was certain the connection was no good. I thought the voices were just messing with me. Then the voices said God wanted to talk to me. I felt they were telling the truth, so I hastily got down on my knees, folded my hands, and put my head on the bed. The sounds I heard were not from this world. I heard the most beautiful music. The sounds seemed to be piped in from heaven. I cannot fully describe the sensation. God said a sentence or two, and I knew everything was going to be okay. But still there would be persecutions. His voice was like running water folded over a man's voice. Nothing of this world could make those sounds. It never happened to me before or since. It was the most beautiful and amazing event that has ever happened to me.

CHAPTER 23

A NEW DRUG

I want to mention how I got addicted hydrocodone. I take
after my mom in addictive traits. She is a chain smoker as
well. My nephew Andrew, Alec's brother, was a hard case. He
was a wannabe gangster and was the "wrong crowd" you hear
tales about. He was about sixteen and it was the Fourth of
July. My mom was over at the house, a duplex we converted
into a large, four-bedroom home. When their parents died,
I left my home farther down the same street and moved in
with them. I didn't want to uproot them. When Rusty died,
the house didn't get paid off and we lived there making
payments for a couple of years. Then it occurred to me to
add a room to my own home and move the boys in there. No
rent or mortgage.

Anyway, Andrew and one of his hoodlum friends walked in
about five o'clock in the morning. I could tell he was spaced
out with no sleep. A girl he had a child by had come over the

night before and said Andrew had ripped her off in a drug deal. I asked him about it, and he denied it. I suspiciously let it slide and told him not to have any drugs in this house. I had previously told him I wouldn't get upset over marijuana, but there could be no white stuff.

I was grilling burgers that day and took a plate into Andrew's room. I didn't knock. He was sitting on his couch with a packet of something white in it. There was a guy trying to buy the stuff from him. We had some words then struggled on the bed for a while. I had Andrew in a body lock and wouldn't let him go. I've seen him kick some ass of much larger people before and knew I was in for a fight. We took it outside.

My mom called the police, but before they arrived he came at me and I connected to his forehead. It didn't even faze him, but I broke my wrist. When the cops arrived, he punched out several windows in the house. I got the cops to leave, and it settled down. He came in and apologized a short time later. He said he would give the drugs back to the dealer.

He was always living on the edge. Twice he had overdosed and we thought we had lost him, but he made it through the hospital stays. The cops and DA knew him well. His juvenile record was long. A month after he turned eighteen, the cops trumped up some charge and got him arrested. It was later dropped, but while out on bail he was exacting revenge on someone for a friend who had gotten jumped the night before. Andrew opened the door to the back of the house, placed his foot on the threshold, and took a swing at the guy. That's all he did—simple assault—but the DA turned it into burglary. He got seven years in prison.

I hope it turns out to be the best thing for him. He calls me often and says he is so sorry for what he put me through. I tell him he can't imagine how minor our interaction was compared to my schizophrenia and not to worry about it. I love him with all my heart. Everything I have will go to him, Alec, and a niece of mine when I pass from this life, which won't be long from now if I believe what the voices tell me. My doctor prescribed pain pills or hydrocodone for my broken wrist. I kept saying I was in pain for about two years. They took hold of me, and they are hard to shake. I try to moderate my consumption but the more I take, the more I need. I've been in prayer about ending this dependency and trust in the Lord that he will strengthen me in the near future and enable me to overcome.

CHAPTER 24

THE PORN

I've put off writing about the events in Tucson that, in part, brought on this disease. I know now that God made me suffer to correct me and bring me home to my family. I have skipped around these chapters trying to delay the inevitable, but I must write it down. The memories I'll be reliving are painful to describe. I believe they are very sinful and self-destructive memories. The kind you try to forget.

I took a break and lay down in my bed for a few minutes while trying to put names to the faces of the people that were around me during these events. I've tried so hard to suppress the memories that I can't recall any of their names. I'll just have to refer to them in pronouns. Not to protect them but because I just can't recall any. I've always been bad with names.

I returned home from Honduras and began immediately submitting a fiancée visa for Alba. I had her get passport photos made to accompany the visa, and she was to get a passport. This is a long, drawn-out process that takes about six to nine months with all the bureaucracy involved.

I figured I had this little time left to enjoy my remaining bachelor days. I got up every morning when I pleased. I had no set time to be at work; as long as I was there for roughly eight hours, my boss was satisfied.

The time spent home when I wasn't traveling became a daily routine of masturbating all afternoon and night while watching porn. The more I watched it, the desire for younger and younger girls affected me. I had searched for younger pornography on my computer and was amazed at what I could find. I spent hours and hours watching the endless videos while pouring Jack and Coke into my belly.

One night I was diving deeper and deeper into the porn, and eventually it got more and more terrible. Finally, skull and crossbones came up on the screen, as if I had been caught by some intelligence agency or a virus. I think it was God stating that I had gone too far.

The next day I bought a new hard drive and destroyed the old one. I was sure the cops would be closing in on me. I wanted to leave no evidence of the porn on my computer.

I had a nice Sony camera and took it with me on all my travels. I took many compromising photos of the girls I knew. I had a whole series on Ligia. I also had a lot from a wild night with a Spanish woman and a friend of hers that was a transvestite, post-op, in Slovakia. I made an account on Yahoo adult groups and posted many of the pics. I also joined many of the groups. I couldn't believe what pics were being posted in every kind of sex group imaginable back then. I even began going to an adult theater for a short period. There was a lot of homosexual activity in there, and I stopped going.

Then I got off from work early one day about 2:00 p.m. The school bus was letting out around the corner of my house. Of course I was masturbating, and I spied this lovely young girl walking around my house on her way home. She lived down the street on my block. I, from then on, tried to get out early from work every day by going in around 5:30 to 6:00 a.m. When I designed my house, I had the best installed: high ceilings, a communication center, and gold-tinted windows to keep the hot Arizona sun out. I don't think the girl every saw me through the half-opened blinds and the tinted windows, but I'm not sure. She might have, because she didn't walk by the house anymore after a couple of weeks.

About three weeks went by and I was driving around my neighborhood. I saw a woman who looked inviting, somewhat desperate. She got in, and she was in bad need of crack cocaine. I didn't know what to do for her. I didn't use and knew of no one to score from. I gave her forty bucks and showed her where I lived, but she never came over.

CHAPTER 25

PROBATION

That got me thinking. I only had a year or so before I was going to get married, so why not do a little before I settle down? I let the idea fade, but it was still present in my thoughts. I lived in a new housing area on the south-central side of Tucson. A pretty tough part of town to live in. I was ending my probation for stabbing a man with a pocketknife that had a three-quarters-inch blade I used to clean my fingernails. It hung on my keychain. I had joined a local member-only bar close to my home and it had a pool league. We would visit area bars for weekly matches. One week we were at a very mean and nasty bar on the south side of Tucson. When we were finished, its champ and I decided to play a game for twenty dollars. I broke and made the eight ball on the break, but my cue ball flew off the table. I was drunk and stunned at this event, and the friend of the guy I played thought I wasn't going to pay up. I was, but I was just stunned for a moment.

All my teammates had left, and I was in their bar alone so I felt boxed in. He got in my face; a struggle ensued. I thought I was going to die, so I pricked his back with the small knife, and blood was everywhere.

It was just a scratch, but the DA made a big deal of it. My buddy Bryon told the DA that I was valedictorian of my high school graduation class of three hundred and fifty. My mom and dad sent letters to the judge. While waiting for trial, I had to get permission from the courts to go to China. Anyway, I got three years of probation.

During this time, I went to a lot of court-ordered AA meetings. The years went by, and I got off probation. About this time the visa finally got Okayed, but Alba was having a lot of trouble with the passport. Officials wanted lots of money to let her escape Honduras, and I can't remember what other issues were involved, but she couldn't leave unless we were married. I wasn't scheduled to go back to Honduras anytime in the foreseeable future. So I said to myself, "The next time I go, I'll marry her, get the passport, and bring her home."

I had noticed my neighbor across the street. She was a beautiful woman with three children. Her boyfriend was in prison. Ray—I think that was his name—was the father of the eldest boy, who was about fifteen. She was a drug addict, and they were struggling in their new home. She had lost her job and wasn't making the house payments anymore. I was in my garage with the door opened and her son came over to borrow something. He asked if I wanted to score any drugs, and I said, "Sure, get me a little crack cocaine and bring it by later tonight." I knew how addictive the drug was from my experience in Corrigan, Texas, but I said, "What the hell."

I started doing it and got addicted again. When you are using drugs, you meet many people who are happy to be with you for what they can get out of you. I used my fair share, but the amount I paid for others was multiple thousands of dollars. I was everyone's friend. I had a little clique of friends that I was around in all my spare time.

CHAPTER 26

SIX MONTHS OF HELL

The entire time from starting back on the pipe to leaving Tucson was about six months. During this short period, I tried to stay in town as much as possible. I know I went to Slovakia once for a two-week period. I went to Mexico about forty times on day trips. I didn't want to be away from the people and drugs.

It didn't take long before the strange things began happening. The woman's boyfriend from across the street was released on probation. We started hanging out. He wasn't supposed to do any drugs on probation and knew he would end up back in prison. But he couldn't resist. There was a never ending supply from me, and he often would say I made him fly.

He was my driver during all the trips to crack houses and hangout spots where people were using. There was this one guy who lived with his mother. He had something like a lean-to in his yard. It was on a normal street but was tucked back a bit, and he had a gated yard. We were pretty safe smoking there.

I never in my life sold drugs to anyone. I was a social user. I gave this guy my supply to sell and said we would split the profits. He smoked it all up, I guess, because he never gave me any money. I stopped going over there.

I had picked up several women from that place. Everyone was down on his or her luck. That's what drugs do to you. I brought one guy over to my house about three months into the ordeal, and he looked around and said, "You still got all this?" He was amazed that I lived in a new home and had many possessions. I gave him a strange look, trying to decipher what that meant. I later realized that doing drugs will take all your possessions away from you, even if you think you're okay and just doing it socially.

I would often buy groceries and toilet paper and necessities of life for people I knew. I once paid a five-hundred-dollar electric bill for a black woman because she had three kids living with her. I would often order pizzas for them and have the driver come to my house after delivery to get paid. At the end of this ordeal, her estranged husband stole my wallet from my back pocket. I had about $1,700 in it because I was preparing to return home to Altus. The garage door was busted at this time and was open about two feet. I was going in the back door, and he grabbed my wallet and made a dash for it. I was on crutches because of my broken heel and couldn't give chase. I called the cops and told them where he lived. They did nothing. It was all part of the disease and the spirits taking everything I had.

I know this for a fact. Spirits were doing so many things to me. They once took fifteen dollars—a ten and a five—out of my wallet while I was sitting on a couch at a drug-addicted female friend's house. I felt them taking it. They were always doing it. They removed it from my wallet, siphoned it through the back of the couch, and were moving it along the floor to eventually get it out of the house though a crack somewhere. I had enough of them taking from me so I pulled back the couch and said to her, "See, I'm not crazy! Here is the money along the wall." I asked her how it could have gotten there through the couch I was sitting on the whole time. She had no answer.

I once had thirty-five dollars in the drawer under my couch at home. It was a large, sectional, custom couch. The spirits had taken the liner off the bottom of the new couch in many areas, and the money five minutes later was gone. I first accused the two girls that were there of taking it. This was a short time before the fifteen-dollar incident on my other friend's couch.

I punished them by some strange means—denying them a hit or something—and then realized what actually had taken place. I had this dog named Perora. That is Spanish for "fart." I got her from someone sharing an apartment with another close female friend. Ray and I would go over there daily. It wasn't far away. We would play cards (rummy) all the time and do the drugs. She had lots of visitors. She was his childhood sweetheart, and he gave her to me one night. She knew I was going through something bad. For all I know, she might have been an angel. She would always carry an open bottle of beer, but she never drank any.

I was telling her of the strange things that were happening to me. A lot of it dealt with tiny beams of light. She made me take a shower to get all the cocaine residue off me, go into her bedroom in total darkness, get under the sheets naked, and stay there for a long while. She said this would make them go away.

Beams of lights still formed from the minor specks of light coming from a street lamp far beyond her window with the shades closed. Nothing could stop them.

Once I was alone in my home. It was daylight, and I completely covered all windows and doors. I had looked out my back patio door, across the yard, and saw a SWAT guy in my neighbor's yard. He was ducking down the brick fencing.

I got a little worried that I was about to be arrested and was trying to smoke what I had left. You see, they would use these lights, any light, and intensify it like a high-powered laser. This wouldn't hurt me, but it would be aimed at the end of the glass crack pipe and make it break. I would often go to the Tanque Verde Swap Meet and buy these pipes by the case.

The light followed me everywhere. I even climbed to the top shelf of my closet and lay down. I had nine-foot ceilings and shut the doors. It still got to the end of the pipe without me even lighting it. I was sure it was some government agency.

Perora was an outside dog, but I would let her in from time to time. Once, I found her holding the remote control in her paws and staring at it. I called her, but she wouldn't break her stare. I glanced at the remote and could see the indicator light coming on and off. I thought she was a real-life mechanical dog and they were programming her.

The girl who brought me home to Altus was living with me at the time, and she got a dog. She said she got it from one of my neighbors. It grew so I knew it was real, and at the same time I thought the government was replacing the dog at intervals to spy on me. I was so sure of this that, even though the girl begged me to take it to the vet and get a Parvo shot, I didn't. It died on the floor of my garage. She cried hysterically and blamed me. I was sure at the time that it was a plant, because it had talked to me. Both dogs had talked to me. I don't recall what they said—a sentence or two about the current situation of what was happening at the time.

I didn't know if this girl was real either. Once she had her twin daughters over and one, so she said, was deathly sick. She wanted me to call an ambulance. I was hip to the tricks of the voices, or government, or spirits, taking all my money, so I said, "I'll drive." I had a fairly new 1999 Monte Carlo I had bought. I said, "We'll take her to the hospital." She said, "No, not the one close by but the one on the other side of Tucson." I didn't give in to the ambulance idea but agreed to go across town. I said, "Get your daughters and get in the car." I drove through the streets of Tucson in record time: sixty miles an hour and running stop lights. I dropped them off at the entrance and got a parking spot. I was only a minute behind them.

I entered the hospital. I searched everywhere for about two hours. They were not there, and no one had seen them. Later, I never asked her about it. I was stupefied, and my thoughts didn't allow me to ask.

CHAPTER 27

THE DEMON FLY

My home was nice. I owned a corner lot with the high, elevated foundation. It had gravel instead of grass and a few plants with an automatic watering system. One day I witnessed a rock of crack that I was about to smoke being sucked into an electrical outlet. I quickly opened it and removed the receptacle to retrieve it. It was just sitting in the bottom of the outlet. As I was reaching for it, it got sucked up the wall. I had an attic and opened the access door. I didn't have any stairs, so I built up a makeshift ladder out of my furniture. It was very shaky. I grabbed on the opening to pull myself up and the furniture fell, so I was just hanging there. I was slim and strong and tried to hoist my body up there. Something was exerting a downward pulling force on my body as I was struggling to get up. I thought, *They don't want me to get up here.* I struggled and struggled 'til I almost passed out. I fell back down, rested a few minutes, and then made a better furniture ladder. Still they tried to keep me out, but I managed to get up there.

It was very hard to find the crack. It looked so much like drywall. I noticed all the insulation had white streaks in it. I plucked some out and said, "A-ha, this is where they've been hiding my stolen drugs." I analyzed it further and noticed the nails coming through my roof were tainted with white. I got back down and went on the roof and noticed white in most of the shingles. Then I noticed white lines leading down the outside of the wall of my house in several locations. Then I noticed the gravel had white specs in about a third of the rocks. I traced it farther, and it had gotten into my automatic watering system so I removed that. I was sure I had found out how the spirits or government drones were making my drugs disappear.

I got a group of people over and had them fill up jars of only the gravel that had large white spots. I was going to try to reclaim my thousands of dollars' worth of drugs they were stealing from me.

But I couldn't get the white out of the rocks and let it go.

I was over at the trailer of this poor girl who I barely knew. I bought a large quantity of drugs, and we were smoking. She didn't say a word the whole time. To get her attention, I took off all my clothes. When she was still speechless, I said I was leaving.

I got really paranoid on the way home. I thought the government or cops were about to arrest me, so I put all the drugs in my mouth during the ride home. It leaked pretty bad and I was getting sick like from an overdose, but not to the point that I was worried. I got home and stashed them in my garage and was waiting for an arrest to happen.

After about twenty minutes, and no one coming over to arrest me, I felt safe and went to retrieve my drugs.

The crack had escaped the baggie and begun marching on the floor, similar to how I envisioned they had been transported to the rocks through my electrical outlet. They were making a beeline to the asphalt seam where the driveway met the garage. There were so many little pieces marching that I could not stop them all. I tried and tried. I then removed the asphalt seam between the concrete slabs. It opened into a subterranean cavity where my plumbing met the sewage. I could see all the plastic tubing opening up to a drain, so I turned on the water hose and made an effort to spray the crack cocaine back into my garage to give me time to collect it.

So many pieces were advancing more rapidly. I spent about forty-five minutes trying in vain to stop it. I finally gave up, and it was all gone. I was late for work, and as amazed as I was, I headed there.

When I got home, I surveyed the situation with my driveway and garage over again. As I was considering what had taken place, I began thinking about all the drugs they had taken from me while I was in the car. I began a close examination of the car. It was a similar situation to the electrical outlet that led to the rocks outside. I wanted to get to the bottom of it and find my drugs that where somewhere in the car. I had a starting point and realized that they were extracting it through the window molding and then down to the tires.

As I stepped back a moment, the car started to go through convulsions. It was bouncing up and down and hunching the driveway concrete like it was trying to eliminate what it still had in it before I located it. I actually watched a car gyrating and moving with no one in it. All this time, there was a grouping of four or more round spots on my garage door windows, as if a power force was using them to reflect onto the car from a helicopter. The ever present helicopter noises were constantly there. It was daylight and I could see none of them, but I believed they were hovering from a range very far away. Sometimes the noise from the helicopters would get really loud like, as if they were hovering over my house.

Then, as I went out to investigate, they would quickly ascend into the air and I couldn't locate the source.

I had screens on all my windows, and for some reason one of my bedroom windows and its screen were open a quarter inch. There were about ten flies in my room. I got my flyswatter and started smacking them. I got them all but one. This one was two and a half times larger than all the rest. I must have swatted at him fifty times. He would always move a split second before I got him. After one attempt, the fly repositioned himself dead center on the top of my mirrored, large nightstand. I looked on in amazement that he wasn't even off by a millimeter. When he was in this spot, I gave a final swat and missed by a split second again. The fly or spirit made a beeline for the quarter-inch opening of the window on the other side of the room and went out. Some guidance system for a fly!

I went out to the backyard. There was a little trash in my personal trashcan but nothing more than usual, and I never had any flies gathered around it. This time there were thousands.

I spent the next hour looking for that fly by swatting nearly all of them. I could not find him.

I was still spending a lot of my time in front of my computer, where I drank heavily and watched porn. I was tweaking over being out of drugs and was naked and searching my carpet for any dropped pieces. This is when I heard the first voice. It said, "Oh, no, Raymond." Then a couple of voices were having a discussion, and they said some name I believe is a heavenly synonym for schizophrenia and pronounced it upon me. It was like they had reached a conclusion and were afflicting me with the disease. I got real sick. I had been awake for six or seven days straight.

I went to my bed to lie down. I started feeling deathly sick and got up and everything was spinning. Lights were coming from everywhere, and they were in many colors. I had complete control of my faculties and knew I was a sane man; I just couldn't understand what was taking place. I went to lie down on my couch. The group of four lights was on my window again, and I closed my eyes for a split second before opening them back up quickly. The flyswatter that had been lying lengthwise on the top of the backrest was now hovering perpendicular to the couch but in the same spot. Just moved in an exact ninety-degree angle to where it had been a split second ago. I reached out and slapped it down.

I had to get out of the house. I jumped in my car around three in the morning and drove. I felt the government closing in on me. Cars were following me. I was at an intersection;

one car was in front of me and one was in back. The first car went through the intersection and pulled over on the side of the road. I wouldn't be followed, so I pulled up behind him a ways back. He then pulled out from the side of the road. I turned and headed down the streets, not knowing where to go. I could hear the helicopters, and then in the distance the helicopters made the lights of a Denny's sign beckon me. They were acting like signal lights. I thought they were setting me up for an arrest, but I went on in anyway.

I ordered something and ate very little. I was suspiciously watching the waitress and cook. No one else was there, and no arrest occurred. Soon I left and headed home.

A deputy sheriff pulled me over for no real reason. I thought, *this is it.*

He just asked a couple of questions and let me go.

I went home and somehow got an hour of sleep before I had to go to work.

A few days before or after this happened, there was a steady stream of cars zipping by my house around two in the morning. I don't mean one or two; I'm talking about thirty to fifty all racing through the neighborhood street at forty-five to fifty miles per hour. It was about this time that I noticed a powdery substance in the air of my home. It was all over me and made me burn with itching. My breathing became hot, and it was like I was breathing in a mist of something. I itched so badly that I took off my clothes and got in the shower. It was in the water as well. I tried to put on clean clothes, but the powdery substance was on all my clothes. It was on all my towels when I tried to dry off. I couldn't breathe.

The girl who lived with me thought I was nuts; she wasn't affected at all. It was all over my bed and throughout the house. I grabbed a blanket and set a chair on my back porch. It still came in waves from the night air. I walked around the block to try to get away from it. Nothing did any good. I went back to my chair on the back porch and looked down the pathway next to the street. There was a brick wall and I could see for about fifteen yards before the curvature of the wall hid my view. I noticed three SWAT team members side by side in a ghostly appearance. My vision was blurred from the substance in the air, and I thought, *Well, this is it.*

I was sure it was three men in uniform, but my vision was blurred badly. They knew I was looking at them, but I don't feel they got the command to invade because they slowly backed up and vanished.

Once I went to light a cigarette and was moving my thumb up to the striker, and the flame appeared. I never touched the striker.

During this period, there were two women that I was a little serious about. Alba was a distant memory by now. One of them had been living with me for a couple of months—not the girl who drove me home. The other was the girl Ray had introduced me to. I had my TV on, and it was tuned to some cartoon. I was in the hallway and trying to take a hit by the laundry room. I was relaxing on top of a pile of dirty clothes. The cartoon seemed to be about my life, and these girls were in it.

I got up and looked around the corner at the TV. I saw a regular, normal cartoon that I had never seen before. I don't recall the actions of the characters, but they were discussing my life. I listened for a while in amazement.

CHAPTER 28

THE FIGHT

I had met this big, black guy. We drove around one day for some reason, but a short time later he brought his ex-con buddy over. He was a thief and was sizing up what he could steal. A day later, the black woman who I had paid the electric bill for said he had sold her my stack of porn DVDs. I bought them back from her. I don't know why I bothered—maybe to help her out—because the entities in my home, the voices in my head, or the government—I didn't know which—had been erasing 80 percent of the movies as I viewed them the first time. I was hitting the fast-forward button to scan the movies to see if they were any good. I had about twenty new ones. The next time I looked at any of them, the content was mostly gone.

The next day, the girl who lived with me had let him in while I was at work. He tried to steal my DVD player but couldn't get it unhooked. I told her to call them or go over to the house he was staying at and tell him I was going to kick his ass. The night before, the TV or the house in general had talked to me, saying he was going to hurt me really bad. The voice was his voice, and it was saying he was going to take what he wanted—everything I owned. Remember I have the reaper on my back and am afraid of no man.

The big black guy I had driven around with a few days prior and the ex-con buddy of his who tried to steal my dvd player came over. I called him into my brick-fenced backyard to have it out. He came at me and I laid him out on the ground with a hard right cross. He got up and I laid him back on the ground again. As I was looking at him on the ground, the big guy hit me on my jaw and knocked me down. I thought he was neutral, but I guess not. I yelled for the girl to call the police and she did. The guy I had decked twice came at me with a metal bar, and I held up my hand in the struggle. He took the meat off my knuckles with it. For some reason, they jumped the fence the moment I got to my feet.

I truly feel the voices or spirits were trying to kill me through these guys. I saw the guy a few days later at one of my favorite places. Both sides of his face were swollen. He never said a word to me or entered my door again. I felt better that I had proved the voices from the house or TV wrong.

CHAPTER 29

MYSTIC BIRDS

I was working on a major project. We had acquired a decrepit old Tiromat packaging machine that was nearly gutted. One mechanic and I were in charge of bringing it back to life. I did all the electrical work and programming on the machine. It was going to be shipped in an ocean-bound container to Slovakia where he and I would install it. We had been given a month to do the work, and I knew my part would take me about a week. I have a very analytical mind. It was a minor job to me.

The company didn't believe we could do it but took a chance on the two of us saving them hundreds of thousands of dollars. They gave us a spending account while in Tucson. Usually I had to travel abroad to get a spending account. We would go to expensive lunches and dinners on the company dime. So to them, it was a very big project.

I ordered all the necessary parts and spent my time writing the program that would make it function. Avent had a large office complex in Tucson. This work took place in our shipping warehouse about a mile away from the office building. The machine was located adjacent to the back door, and I would often go outside to take breaks. The helicopters were constantly hovering, and I would go outside to try to spot them. I thought that at any moment they would be dropping a SWAT team on the roof.

I would lie down on my back outside to peer into the sky easier. I started noticing birds and butterflies that were not real but were flying in direct paths over my line of sight. I tried to figure out where they were coming from, and there was a vacant field near the warehouse. These birds looked very real, but they never flapped their wings. I thought they were spy drones and someone was controlling them in the field. I was looking in the direction of the field and saw what I thought was a man peering over the tall shrubs. I raced over there, but no one was there. There was a new four-wheel drive truck about a half mile away in the field where it shouldn't be, but there was no sign of anyone.

I went back to work and was trying to tighten some terminals where I had done some wiring. The terminal was definitely loose, but it was locked frozen in its' open position. So I tried another one, and the same thing occurred. I tried to tighten it with all my might, and it started glowing red. There was no electric power on this machine at the time. I couldn't understand why the government would be doing this to me.

The next day, I headed for work and stopped at a convenience store for coffee. I felt I was being tailed. A car pulled up next to where I had parked. I had already gone in but was watching my car intently. I tried to keep drugs and paraphernalia out of my car but remembered a girl had left her pipe in the backseat. The car had about seven people wearing suits and sunglasses. I was getting my coffee, and three of them came in. I felt they were watching me. I looked out the window, and a woman that was with them had a blue scanning pen in her hand. I could see her moving it over my back window. I thought for sure this was it.

I paid for my coffee, got in my car, and drove off.

They didn't follow me, and I was only a couple of miles from the warehouse. I was astonished and a little frightened.

CHAPTER 30

THE CASTLE OF BLOOD

We completed the project and had to wait a couple of weeks for it to get across the ocean to be delivered to our plant in Slovakia. I had been there many times and looked forward to going back. I knew I couldn't score any drugs there and also knew I couldn't take any. It was going to be a little rough on me, because doing drugs had become a routine.

I left my new car in my neighbor's garage and allowed a couple of girls to stay in my house while I was gone. I called my house from Slovakia, and one of them convinced me to let her use my car. When I came back, it was in the impound yard and badly damaged. My super nice golf clubs had been pawned for about thirty bucks by someone to get some crack. I had Western Unioned them some money. They were letting my house be used by anyone.

My mom, who didn't know I was out of the country, visited Tucson from Altus. She was upset with Willy. She just got in her van and drove to my home. The girls who were staying in my home let her in, and my mom later asked me why the electrical outlets were all opened up. I told her I was installing a PLC in my home. I was doing that, but that was not the real reason the outlets were dismantled. I think we all know why. She stayed a couple of days and could sense something was wrong.

The nightlife in Piestany, Slovakia, was great. I had a friendship with the two girls who worked at the bed-and-breakfast I often stayed at. Once, before I met Alba, I was getting serious with one of them, but she liked someone else. I did all I could to get her to fall in love with me, but she would have none of it. We went out a lot but had no sex. I was telling the other one about it, and she could sense my despair. This other one was drop-dead gorgeous with a perfect body. She said if the other one didn't sleep with me, she would. That lifted my spirits.

I made my pilgrimage to the Castle of Blood. I knew the back route up the mountain through a narrow side street of the town on the east side of the mountain. Legend has it that the countess of the castle blood let over five hundred local virgins to their death in order to bathe in their blood. The locals of the town eventually tore down most of the castle and killed her.

I went to the castle every time I visited Piestany. It was about ten miles away from Piestany directly above the town of Chactice. The background image currently on my computer shows a picture I took of it from a couple of hundred yards away. It is a famous place, and there have been documentaries about it on TV.

I was at the spot on the mountain, about to exit the car and go to the castle, when I began crying uncontrollably. I wanted the girls' love so much. It was hopeless. This was a few weeks before meeting Alba in Honduras and well before the schizophrenia and drug use began. I needed to find a wife soon.

Maybe some spirits from the castle entered me on that visit. When I returned from the Slovakian trip of installing the Tiromat machine, my car was in the impound yard. I got it out, but it was nearly totaled. I called my insurance agent and he deemed it totaled. I got a few thousand dollars for the damages and swore I wouldn't loan it out again. I had to get a new title for it as a wrecked car. There were legal issues for keeping it on the road in the condition it was in.

CHAPTER 31

WICCANS

I began using again, and it was near Christmastime. I took a vacation from work. I used up two weeks of my vacation during this period so I had three and a half weeks away from work when you add in the days the company gave us off for Christmas.

I partied as usual but wasn't sleeping much, so the parties lasted for longer periods. One female friend that I was pretty close to, but never had sex with, thought she had the perfect female for me. She thought she was just what I was looking for. She was a beautiful, petite blonde who was about twenty-five years old. I thought, *Tonight is my night.* She made the introductions and left my house.

We began partying and doing shotgun transfers (mouth-to-mouth exchanges of the crack smoke). She told me she was a Wiccan. I wasn't positive what she meant. I had heard the term used before but wanted to know from her what she meant. She explained a few things and said Wiccans use sex to get what they want. I got my clothes off, cozied up into my bed, and invited her in. Then out of the blue, I asked, "You're not married, are you?" She said, "Yes, I am." That changed everything. I remained in bed with my clothes off but decided, *No way am I gonna burn in hell for adultery*.

I remind the voices all the time of that night. The entities in my house or the voices at that time seemed destined to make me commit adultery. I had this big, thick comforter, and I wrapped myself up in it and went to the window in my paranoid state to see who was in my backyard. I was just looking out the window and felt a strong force pulling the comforter down to expose my nakedness. I fought the comforter for a couple of minutes but could not keep it around my body. It dropped to the floor. I didn't give in though. The Holy Spirit within me wouldn't let me do that sin that night.

This couple needed a place to stay. I had met them over at a friend's house. I converted my computer room into a bedroom. I had previously been converting it to a bedroom for the two children of one of the girls who stayed with me off and on. I bought new bunk beds for the two children. The children never moved in, so I let them use the room. This guy seemed very intelligent. I would imagine his IQ was pretty high. The kind of guy who is an evil jack-of-all-trades.

The human resources woman at Avent, Kimberly Clark, knew something was not right with me and held a couple of meetings with my supervisor and me. She was giving me a stern warning to clean up my act. I wasn't too concerned. My boss had recently introduced me to his new boss by stating I was the best programmer in Kimberly Clark. That was a huge compliment. I couldn't believe he held me in that high of regard. He had been an engineer with KC for over twenty years. He knew of many electrical engineers. I was sure my job was safe.

One night my latest girlfriend came over and was cooking me dinner. That was a rare treat. We were going to eat and spend the night doing drugs and having wild sex. I thought we would be alone, but the couple living with me came over. I asked them to leave so we could be alone. The guy asked me to go into the garage to talk. I said no. I wanted him to leave. He then stated, "This girl is only here to steal everything from you." I didn't think so, and the talks got heated. I ended up hitting him in the jaw with a right cross.

He called the cops, and I was arrested. In my paranoid state, I had locked the doors to every room. The cops took note of that and had me sitting in the back seat of the patrol car.

They took a long time and had the trunk open. I was sure they had a drug-residue detection device on my seat. The police officer told me I could not go back to my house for ten days. I later found out they had no authority to say that, but I didn't know it at the time. It may very well have been the voices I hear making the words come out of the cop's lips.

I was booked on assault. I was in the holding tank and tried to make a call to work the next morning to try to keep my job. Nothing I did would work. I couldn't complete the call. I was sitting in the tank, and I could hear the voice of the guy I had hit coming over the intercom system. He was saying disturbing things to me. I now know it was the voices playing tricks on me, but at the time I grew more paranoid. I thought he was an undercover cop. About a week before, the cops had been over to my house while I was at work. The girl that was living with me called them regarding this guy. I left my office and pulled up. I was listening to the guy talk to the cops, and he was spitting out a bunch of code letters and numbers to the officer. They meant, "You can't arrest me. I'm an undercover agent."

They released me that morning, and I walked to a sleazy motel. I was told I couldn't go home, so I rented a room for a week. I had been informed that I was fired.

CHAPTER 32

GIVE ME YOUR WALLET

I called one of my drug suppliers and was just relaxing in the room. I met a young woman coming out of another room and struck up a conversation. At this time, I was out of drugs and in a great deal of pain from my broken heel. She had some, so she came over. We got on the bed and were making out. I thought, *Where is this gonna lead?* She convinced me to go to the local convenience store and get some cash so we would score some more drugs. She went with me, and I could sense she was trying to get my pin number.

We returned and she went to get the guy who she said had the supply. He came into my room and put a gun to my head while demanding the money. I gave him my wallet, and they left. I couldn't do anything. My foot was broken, and I was on crutches because two days earlier I had dropped from a bridge to collect the crack pipe I had thrown away. I was in excruciating pain.

I called the cops.

They took one look at me and figured it was a drug deal and told me I shouldn't have been here and left.

I was lying in the bed of the hotel and watching porn while the voices were sending me all kinds of thoughts and talking to me. They seemed to be grabbing my heel and twisting it to increase my pain level.

The next morning, I got the Bible out of the nightstand and started reading. I did this for a couple of days. I then had the thought that I should now go home. I took a cab and limped up to my door. It was one quarter opened.

I went in and saw the girl who stayed with me, the one who drove me home to Altus, was there. Almost all my possessions were gone. I asked her why she let this happen. I couldn't understand how she could just let people take everything. She had said she loved me. I found out it was a free-for-all. Two different groups of people had been raiding my home. My latest girlfriend's friends and the guy I had punched both had crews removing things. I'm talking new king-sized beds in all the rooms, appliances, TVs, etc. They took my custom-made silk robe I had been given as a gift from the plant supervisor in gratitude for fixing his major problem in five minutes. Of course it was a twelve-hour, first-class trip to and from China. They also stole my collection of various Budweiser bottles from different countries. They stole everything. I didn't know what to do or where to turn.

I had a little clock radio and just lay on the living room floor for a few days while listening to the current songs from a weird but calming station. The hit list brought me to my senses. My car had been stolen as well. I was lying there the first night, and a group of three guys opened the garage door. They had backed up a truck to load up what remained. I jumped up, but what could I do on crutches? They opened the back entranceway, saw me, and high-tailed it out of there.

The black woman who I had given many things to came over with a friend of hers. We partied a little with their supply of drugs. I was dead broke and was about $20,000 in debt with my credit cards. I got very friendly with the new friend. She was a beautiful black woman. She said her mom had my kitchen table, and she would give it back. She also said she could take me to where most of my stuff was, and I could get it all back. I said, "No. I think it was meant to be."

I called my mom and asked if I could return home. The next day, as luck would have it, a man was canvassing the neighborhood in search of houses to buy. He said he would pay off my mortgage and give me a thousand dollars for my home. I happily agreed. I hadn't made a mortgage payment in five months. This was a few years before the housing crisis began.

CHAPTER 33

LEAVING TUCSON FOR GOOD

I've now described most of the high points of the crises I endured during the final six months in Tucson. A whole lot more happened that I could add, but I will leave that to your imagination. I may be able to elaborate further on some details for those who wish to e-mail me.

I did come back to my house in Tucson few months later. My cousin Danny and I made the trip. I was going to get my car. I had been notified that it was in the impound yard for the third time. I paid the fees and got the keys back. My four wheels were gone. I had expensive custom mag wheels with brand-new Michelin tires, and they were gone.

We went to a store where I bought a cheap set of four wheels and tires. We put them on and drove back to my place. The agency that was buying my house hadn't taken possession yet. The electricity was still on, and the girl was still staying there.

I realized the fifteen- to twenty-mile trip had taken well over half a tank of gas. I surmised the controlling computer chip for the car had been removed. I couldn't afford the gas home, so I gave it to someone.

I met again the man I had punched in my home. He and a former girlfriend of mine were walking down a side street near my home. This took place after I had returned to Tucson with Danny to collect what remained in my garage. I had put the break-in behind me and thought he had done what he did because he was either a rogue undercover cop or influenced by the spirits.

I drove up to the intersection that they were approaching. I rolled my window down, not sure what I would say to them.

He skittishly approached, and I held out my hand in a gesture showing it was over and I had no hard feelings for what he had done. Then I drove off without saying a word to them.

I headed back to my empty home and told Danny, "I'm ready to get the hell out of here."

I haven't been back to Tucson since then. Danny met a few of my friends and said he wanted to stay. There were a lot of good times to be had with those people, but I convinced him we had to return.

CHAPTER 34

GOD'S BLESSINGS

Today my day-to-day activities are pretty mundane. I rise with the first rays of sunshine coming through my window and generally go to sleep around nine o'clock at night. Sometimes, I wake up in the middle of the night from a colorful dream and can't get back to sleep. On many of these occasions, I get in my new car and drive sixty miles to Lawton to hit the casino. It has a realistic video blackjack machine that often pays me out pretty nice. I bet relatively big. I almost always win a couple hundred dollars at a time. The experience I've gained from the many times I've played blackjack and lost is starting to pay off. I find it exhilarating and the voices don't bother me there either.

I return home by 7:30 a.m. to do my daily tasks. I visit my mom and cook breakfast for my nephew. I then clean up the house a little and browse auction sites to pick up good deals on fine art. I then manage my store on eBay.

Throughout the day, I watch lots of television. I hate commercials and always mute them. The voices chime in immediately when I press mute. They only slightly annoy me while I'm watching a TV program, so I tend to watch premium channels with no interruptions.

TV gets boring, and I can only stand so much, so most of my day is spent listening to the ramble from the voices. It keeps me somewhat entertained, but I hate the confusion.

There are many bridges to pass on my way to and from Lawton. On them, I always say prayers for those I know. I seldom ask anything for myself. God meets all my needs except Alba being my wife.

Alba is a constant prayer request. I ask God to bless her with a fine husband who loves Jesus first and Alba with all his heart. The voices tell me she is still single and waiting for my return. After the fiasco at the airports, I made a vow that I would not go to Honduras to get her unless God sent prepaid tickets to my mailbox. I feel this is the only means by which I can know for sure that God wants her to be with me as my wife. And when I'm mentally ready, he will do this for me.

I cannot have a relationship and schizophrenia at the same time, so I've resolved to wait upon the Lord until this passes. I do not want to tempt the Lord but have resolved that without him sending me tickets, I will not ever go. The voices have taken so much from me that I will not be duped again.

I'm hoping and praying that she is okay. I still love her now as much as the day I brushed her hair, but my hands are tied. She probably hates me for abandoning her, and I can't blame her. If she ever reads this book, maybe she will understand. I want to share the news of some of my blessings. I can't believe them.

As you know, when I returned from Tucson I had almost nothing and was deep in debt. I believe all these many blessings are the result of doing God's will. Alec and I get plenty of cash from our social security checks and his dad's retirement checks. It's enough to easily pay our bills and help others. I have a solid-gold Rolex watch; a ten-gram, eighteen-karat gold, one-karat weight, VSS-clarity diamond ring; a heavy, fourteen-karat-gold rope necklace with a heavy, fourteen-karat-gold crucifix; a customized 1966 Chevy stepside truck with a .350 engine that just purrs; a Ford Ranger; and a new Mazda 3. I had a Toyota 4Runner four-wheel drive. It was a 1995 model and was fully loaded. The sticker was still in the glove box. It cost $33,500 new in 1995. It was garage kept all these years and only had 52,000 miles on it. I got it for $2,500 cash. I owned it for four years and put 25,000 miles on it, and then Jerry Don needed it for his work. He is a mason. I felt it was still worth $5,000 to $7,000 but let him have it for $5,000 in cash and trade.

We own four houses with no mortgages and approximately $350,000 worth of fine art. I have a gold and silver coin collection that I value well over $25,000. I have a high credit rating. I have five credit cards having a zero balance at the end of each month. We have $50,000 in a high-dividend stock that adds $250 a month to my checking account and six or seven suits. I have a tuxedo as well. I don't know how well this book will sell, but I expect some royalties coming from it.

I have three dogs that I love very much. I got Lisa, which was my deceased sister's name, when she was a couple of weeks old. I got her two weeks after my sister died. I feel there is a kinship with my sister through my dog. She is a Boston terrier. I've had her for about six years now. I took in a small stray mutt. They both sleep in my bed, and I cater to their every need. I have a German shepherd protecting my yard where I have a large storage shed packed with possessions.

I have the love and company of my many family members who I was away from for so long. I have my church and a quiet peaceful city in which to dwell. I have three phones, the full package of DirecTV, four computers, and the latest large-screen TVs in every room. All this and I don't have to get up and go to work as I've done all my life. These things were given to me for just obeying God's will and following Jesus. I try to give away as much as I can, but the good Lord blesses me with three times as much soon after I give to those who need it. I don't really want any of this stuff, except my dogs, but the more I give it away, the more God blesses me.

CHAPTER 34

WILL IT END

I finished writing the first draft of this manuscript this morning, which is June 13, 2012. I had been up since 3:00 a.m. I made my morning drive to my mother's apartment. I focused my thoughts toward the voices to hear from them regarding having completed the book. I could barely hear them. They were still present but muted to a large degree. I cannot make out what they were mumbling.

I thought perhaps this ordeal was ending. Later this afternoon, I returned home from lunch with my nephew. I was finished with the book and had made an editing change or two. I was saving the changes. The book was finished, and I was saving it to my backup drive. For some reason, I deleted the file from my backup before I copied the latest file from my computer. The file I was saving on my computer then vanished. The voices or powers that be were up to their old tricks. Maybe they didn't like it? Possibly they just wanted to harass me and make me rewrite it.

Luckily I did find a backup from a few days prior. I know how to handle files and did not make a mistake in saving the file. It just vanished. Maybe this ordeal is far from over. Am I in hell?

In closing, the main thing I want to say to anyone who is suffering from this disease is this: charity and love cover a multitude of sins! God will pour out blessings you cannot contain if you have love and charity in your heart. One of those blessings might be a form of schizophrenia that you will be able to cope with. Give your tithes to the church, and give until it hurts. God will meet your needs, so take the chance, give, and watch what happens. Forgive the people who offend you.

I love you all and I say to you "Give your life over to Jesus. You will have persecutions, but you must pass this life test. Your time here on earth is miniscule compared to an eternity in either hell or heaven. Read your Bible daily, put it in your heart, and act on what you've read."

God bless you all, and farewell, my friends.

ABOUT THE AUTHOR

Raymond Edgell has begun living a lifestyle that has helped him cope with the horrific disease of schizophrenia. He feels he knows the only cure.

Ray is desperately waiting for this disease to recede. He feels this is the only way he can triumphantly return to the foreign country where the love of his life lives and ask her again to marry him. He desires to bring her home to the quiet, little town of Altus, in southwest Oklahoma, where they can enjoy and share their lives.

Ray is a fine art dealer who has a store on eBay called Ray's Fine Art and More, username steadyy. He spends his days buying and selling art. He also cares for his dogs and does things for his family. His young nephew lives with him. Ray tries to maintain the home and make him happy.